The Los Angeles Coffee Guide.

2018

D1455440

Edited by
Jeffrey Young

Author: Allegra Strategies
Project Manager: Samantha Hughes
Project Assistant: Hannah Hill
Reviews and Data Collection: Lauren Tisza, Jeffrey Young,
Maggie Cadden, John Imhoff and Haley Evans
Photography: Tyler Nix, Horst A. Friedrichs, Chérmelle D. Edwards
and provided by venues
Design: John Osborne
Website: Tim Spring
Publisher: Allegra Publications Ltd

Allegra
PUBLISHING

Visit our website:
www.losangelescoffeeguide.com

 @losangelescoffeeguide

All information was accurate at time of going to press.

Published by Allegra Publications Ltd © 2018

Serendipity House, 106 Arlington Road, London, NW1 7HP, UK.

Foreword

by **Yeekai Lim**, Founder, Cognoscenti Coffee

I moved to Los Angeles in 2005 to further my architecture education and practice, and shortly thereafter opened my studio in lower Manhattan, New York. The projects dwindled in 2008, which brought me back to LA during the Intelligentsia launch. I didn't realize I had been drinking years of bad coffee until I had my first cup there, and it was this that inspired my coffee mission. It started with the pop-up serving multiple roasters, and led to me teaming up with Na Young from Proof Bakery as we embarked on a search for quality both in pastries and in coffee. In 2012, I opened the modest 400 square foot coffee shop in the Culver City Arts District, on the ground floor of Clive Wilkinson's Studio. Fast forward six years and we now have three shops; the last of which, located in DTLA's fashion district, houses the exciting new addition of a Probat UG15. The next chapter of our mission has begun.

At Cog, we deeply respect and cherish our local community, for we realize none of us would be where we are without their support. Diversity has enriched our city, bringing with it empowered talent and rooted beginnings. Pop-ups are nothing new to the City of Angels, where mobile kitchens and food trucks thrive on every street corner. This may be, in part, due to the strict regulations and permitting requirements for opening restaurants, but we are grateful to be a part of the city fabric. The coffee scene here is also nothing short of constant experimentation and creativity, especially in coffee brewing and shop designs.

Over the past decade, our community has forged stronger connections between importers and farmers, resulting in tremendous improvements in both the quality and the ethical sourcing of coffee. Knowing how much effort goes into each cup, I have become very sensitive to coffee waste, and here at Cog we are proud to implement a low waste approach of dialing in. As new roasters emerge in LA, I look forward to the dialogue growing ever stronger and more meaningful, addressing issues of sustainability and re-use. I see coffee shops working more closely to restaurant industry standards as well as increasing access to better quality coffee in restaurants. I am optimistic about where coffee is headed and especially so in Los Angeles, where I will always strive to meet the Gold standard.

Contents

Introduction

Welcome to The Los Angeles Coffee Guide 2019 - the definitive guide to Los Angeles' best specialty coffee destinations.

The Los Angeles Coffee Guide is a brand-new book that aims to inspire LA visitors and natives alike to explore the flourishing coffee scene and all the exquisite craft coffee venues that the city has to offer. With a focus on the true crème de la crème of coffee destinations, we hope to guide you and your taste buds to some of the best coffee in LA.

In this book you will find 110 of the very best coffee shops in LA. We have included a 'Noteworthy' stamp on venues we feel merit a special mention. We have also included a 'Top 40' stamp for the venues that truly stand out for their impressive coffee and overall excellence, and a 'Top 10' for the absolute superstar venues. We would like to thank all who have contributed.

The 5th Wave of coffee has become well and truly established in Los Angeles, with independent specialists adopting a boutique-at-scale approach to coffee and opening multiple sites with their winning recipe for success, whilst still retaining their unique character and high quality.

Allegra Strategies is an established leader in research and business intelligence for the coffee industry. We have drawn on this research as well as a variety of other sources to compile The Los Angeles Coffee Guide. We hope you enjoy it!

Photo: Horst A. Friedrichs

About the Guide

Every venue featured in The Los Angeles Coffee Guide 2019 has been visited by our expert team. We have two levels of ranking within the guide, both highlighted with a stamp: Top 40, and Top 10. The Top 40 are the venues that we feel bring something special to the coffee scene and are truly standout destinations for great coffee. The Top 10 are superstar venues that are an absolute must-visit. Customer and industry feedback also inform the venue shortlist and the Top 40 & Top 10.

Key to symbols

In-store roastery		Disabled access	
Alternative brew methods available		Credit cards accepted	
Decaffeinated coffee available		WiFi available	
Coffee beans sold on site		Alcohol served	
Gluten-free products available		Coffee courses available	
Venue has a loyalty card		Outdoor seating	
Milk alternatives available		Brunch available at weekends	
Restrooms		Cold brew available	
Parent & baby friendly		Computer friendly	

Venues marked as are venues that we feel are worthy of special mention.

Venue List

DTLA &
Chinatown

Bardonna

724 South Spring Street, CA 90014 | **DTLA**

Nestled at the front of the popular Corporation Food Hall sits Bardonna, a small coffee and food bar with espresso from Mad Lab. Try the Columbian espresso and find hints of strawberry - the acidity balances out the berry flavors beautifully. An iced nitro brew with condensed milk and honey is also a must try item; it's lightly sweet and creamy, making it a great option for those with a slight sweet tooth. The baristas are friendly and knowledgeable and are sure to make your daily experience at Bardonna a great one.

(213) 221-7087
www.bardonna.com

Sister locations Larchmont Village / Santa Monica / Brentwood / WKNDR

MON-SUN.   7:00am - 5:00pm

First opened 2017
Roaster Mad Lab Coffee
Machine La Marzocco GB5 EE, 2 groups
Grinder Fiorenzato F64 EVO

Espresso	$3.50
Cappuccino	$4.50
Latte	$5.00
Cold brew	$4.50

Best Girl Coffee Counter at Ace Hotel

929 South Broadway, CA 90015 | **DTLA**

DTLA & Chinatown

Positioned in the front lobby of LA's infamous Ace Hotel is a small, yet prominent corner coffee shop called Best Girl, the hotel's premier coffee destination. Stumptown coffee is on bar and brings a delicious cup of Joe to everyone who orders. Bringing your own mug to Best Girl gets you your drip coffee for a dollar, however the espresso options are delicious and shouldn't be passed up. Whether you're staying at Ace or not, Best Girl is a lovely spot to stop and relax with a great cup of coffee.

(213) 235-9660
www.bestgirldtla.com

MON-SUN.   6:00am - 9:00pm

First opened 2014
Roaster Stumptown Coffee Roasters
Machine La Marzocco GB5 EE, 2 groups
Grinder Mazzer Luigi Super Jolly E

Espresso	$3.00
Cappuccino	$5.00
Latte	$5.00
Cold brew	$4.00

6

No. 2

Blue Bottle Coffee Arts District

582 Mateo Street, CA 90013 | **Arts District**

This Bay Area-based operator made its Los Angeles debut in the Arts District, former home to Handsome Coffee Roasters. In its day, Handsome was the foremost coffee destination in the city, and this takeover is testament to the immense influence Blue Bottle now has across the LA coffee scene. This roastery/café is a pillar for local operations as the sole roasting location for the growing set of LA cafés. In fact, one of the first things you'll notice on entering is the rich coffee aroma wafting through from the roastery in the back of the shop. Every espresso shot pulled here is notably delicious, and any variant of the menu will leave you handsomely satisfied. Perfectly central to the best that the LA Arts District has to offer, Blue Bottle is a shop you wouldn't want to miss.

(510) 653-3394
bluebottlecoffee.com

MON-SUN.   6:30am - 6:00pm

First opened 2014
Roaster Blue Bottle Coffee
Machine La Marzocco FB80, 2 groups
Grinder Mazzer Luigi Robur

Espresso	$3.50
Cappuccino	$4.50
Latte	$5.00
Cold brew	$4.00

Sister locations Multiple locations

Blue Bottle Coffee Bradbury

300 South Broadway, CA 90013 | **DTLA**

The Los Angeles flagship location of Blue Bottle is beyond magnificent with its high vaulted ceilings, sleek minimalist design, and wide-open space. Ideally located at the heart of Downtown, this rapidly expanding brand truly outdoes itself with this café. All the regular Blue Bottle menu options are available here, with the added benefit of a truly exceptional and spacious atmosphere. The pour overs are the definition of classic, with each cup made under the watchful 'eye' of Blue Bottle's tried and true brewing perimeters. Look to the bar and you will see the various brew methods beautifully laid out and awaiting you, siphons and pour overs glistening. As if there weren't enough reasons to visit this incredible location, it also houses Blue Bottle's first library, so you can buy a good novel to read while you sip that perfect pour over. It also has an impressive Cold Bar, unique to this outpost of Blue Bottle, which is a zero-proof bar where baristas create spectacular cocktail-esque concoctions with beautiful cold brew, Oji and single origin coffees. This DTLA shop is an important addition to your Los Angeles list of must-dos.

MON-SUN.   6:30am - 6:00pm

First opened 2016
Roaster Blue Bottle Coffee
Machine La Marzocco GB5, 3 groups
Grinder Mazzer Luigi Robur

Espresso	$3.50
Cappuccino	$4.50
Latte	$5.00
Cold brew	$4.00

(510) 653-3394
bluebottlecoffee.com

Sister locations Multiple locations

Café Dulce Dos

777 South Alameda Street #150, CA 90021 | **DTLA**

Part bakery and part café, Dulce is a great spot to relax with coffee and pastry in hand. Ordering a latte will result in a truly beautiful cup, and the latte art produced here is phenomenal. The espresso from Heart has a great taste, and ordering a cappuccino or macchiato really brings out the unique flavor notes. Expect attentive service along with great food, making this a perfect spot to enjoy your delicious order every time you stop by.

(213) 536-9633
www.cafedulce.co

Sister locations Little Tokyo

MON–SUN.   8:00am – 5:00pm

First opened 2014
Roaster Heart Coffee Roasters
Machine Slayer Espresso V3, 3 groups
Grinder Compak

Espresso	$3.00
Cappuccino	$3.75
Latte	$4.50
Cold brew	$4.25

Café Integral at Freehand Los Angeles

416 West 8th Street, CA 90014 | **DTLA**

Photo: Patrick Chin

This little café is charming and classy; stunning wood accents and thoughtful design makes it feel cozy, yet harmoniously put together. This Café Integral outpost is incorporated into the hotel lobby of the Freehand Hotel, and the stunning design of the hotel is brought flawlessly into the café space. Nicaraguan coffees are its niche - smooth, balanced, and packed with flavor, the espresso shines no matter what variation of it you order. The cappuccino is especially of note, bringing out the espresso's delicious aroma and showcasing Café Integral's commitment to crafting delicious coffee.

freehandhotels.com/los-angeles/
cafe-integral/

MON-SUN.   6:00am - 2:00pm

First opened 2017
Roaster Café Integral
Machine La Marzocco Linea PB, 3 groups
Grinder Compak F10, Compak R120

Espresso	$3.00
Cappuccino	$4.00
Latte	$4.50
Cold brew	$4.00

Café Société

1802 Industrial Street #260, CA 90021 | **Arts District**

Formerly The Daily Dose, this café is eclectic and cozy with exposed brick and reclaimed wood being the dominant design details inside. Step out into the alley to take a seat and soak up some California sunshine. The baristas are warm and welcoming and are sure to help you order a coffee you'll love. Café Société uses Stereoscope beans to deliver a full-bodied depth of flavor that'll drive any coffee lover wild. Go for a fragrant pour over to fully appreciate the complexity of the roast. The colorful outdoor seating is plentiful and perfect for spending a beautiful afternoon in good company or alone on a laptop.

(213) 935-8189
societe.cafe

Sister locations Es Todo

MON.	Closed
TUE-SUN.	8:00am – 4:00pm

First opened 2012
Roaster Stereoscope Coffee
Machine Synesso Cyncra, 2 groups
Grinder Mazzer Luigi

Espresso	$4.00
Cappuccino	$5.00
Latte	$5.50

Coffee Hall

970 North Broadway #112, CA 90012 | **Chinatown**

Coffee Hall makes craft coffee simple and sweet in a space pared down to the essentials. Delectable espresso is the name of the game here. The goal of co-founder Aldo Lihiang was to create something special for the Chinatown community. The entire premise of the shop is based upon guests setting up and running Coffee Hall like it's their own. Shops like La Colombe, Smith & Tate, Sightglass Roasters and Devoción have been some of the 40 coffee shops that have come through Coffee Hall in a year and half. The espresso rotates as quickly as the featured coffee shops do, which creates the most rich and diverse experience possible for the regular patron. You'll always have something new to try here, and new people to meet - oftentimes people at the top of their game in the craft coffee world.

(213) 328-7575
www.hellomooon.com/coffee-hall/

MON-SUN. 9:00am - 5:00pm

First opened 2016
Roaster Multiple rotating roasters
Machine Sanremo Café Racer, 2 groups
Grinder Mahlkönig K30, Mahlkönig EK 43

Espresso	Varies
Cappuccino	Varies
Latte	Varies
Cold brew	Varies

Sister locations Lately

Cognoscenti Coffee South Park

868 South Olive Street, CA 90013 | **DTLA**

Cognoscenti creates an artisanal experience for its customers with finely-tuned espresso as well as an ultra-modern interior design. Bright lighting, dark colored walls, light wood shelving, and marble counters all aid to create its thoroughly enjoyable ambiance. Even the seating is beautifully thought through, and there is a perfect perch for any occasion, whether working at a table or relaxing on a woven stool and socialising with friends. The nitro cold brew is smooth and rich, and the iced vanilla lattes are a local popular favorite. Taste the full flavor profile of Cog's own beans by choosing a flawlessly executed espresso. Deeply conscious of the waste in the coffee industry, founder, Yeekai Lim, has implemented a low waste policy in all Cognoscenti locations. Plan to stay a while - this feel-good environment is hard to leave behind.

MON-SUN. 7:00am - 7:00pm

First opened 2016
Roaster Cognoscenti Coffee
Machine La Marzocco Linea PB, 2 groups,
Kees van der Westen Spirit, Mavam
Grinder Mahlkönig EKK 43, Compak E10,
Mazzer Luigi Kony, Nuova Simonelli

Espresso	$3.00
Cappuccino	$4.00
Latte	$4.50
Cold brew	$4.00

(213) 263-3349
www.cogcoffee.com

Sister locations Culver City /
Fashion District

Demitasse

135 South San Pedro Street, CA 90012 | **Little Tokyo**

This location in Little Tokyo is a great place to spend an afternoon. Demitasse was started by a coffee-loving former lawyer who left his law practice in favor of making his own unique impression on the Los Angeles coffee scene. The Cubano, a drink with sugar, mint leaves, espresso, and milk shaken over ice, is a year-round customer favorite. The baristas at this café see coffee as an opportunity to put on a show for their patrons, creating entertainment by bringing flair to their coffee making. If you're looking for a unique coffee experience, Demitasse Little Tokyo is the café for you.

(323) 844-3233
cafedemitasse.com

Sister locations Santa Monica / Mid-Wilshire / West Hollywood

MON-FRI.	7:00am - 7:00pm
SAT-SUN.	8:00am - 7:00pm

First opened 2011
Roaster Demitasse Coffee Roasters
Machine La Marzocco Strada, 2 groups
Grinder Nuova Simonelli Mythos Clima Pro

Espresso	$3.50
Cappuccino	$4.15
Latte	$4.50
Cold brew	$4.00

16

Endorffeine

727 North Broadway #127, CA 90012 | **Chinatown**

Simplicity meets delicious craft coffee in this unique Chinatown café destination. Despite its ultra-minimalist interior, Endorffeine has everything it needs to give you a spectacular coffee experience. The menu is simple and straight to the point, as Endorffeine allows its espresso to be the central focus of its menu. Featuring Heart Roasters, Coffee Collective, and other rotating guest roasters, you're sure to find a flavor profile that suits your unique tastes. Bring a book and plan to stay a while - the atmosphere is quiet and calm, making it a great place to relax or get work done. Order a cortado, expertly crafted on the stunning Modbar, and enjoy the zen.

endorffeine.coffee

MON.	Closed
TUE-FRI.	7:00am - 6:00pm
SAT-SUN.	8:00am - 4:00pm

First opened 2015
Roaster Drop Coffee Roasters, Coffee Collective, Heart Coffee Roasters and guests
Machine Modbar, 2 groups
Grinder Mahlkönig EK 43, Mazzer Luigi Robur E

Espresso	$3.25
Cappuccino	$3.75
Latte	$4.50
Cold brew	$4.00

G&B

317 South Broadway #6, CA 90013 | **DTLA**

G&B, the Downtown Los Angeles flagship store for owners Kyle Glanville and Charles Babinski, is an incredible demonstration of good old-fashioned hospitality with a modern twist. Take a seat anywhere on the rectangular bar and be met with a friendly welcome and a menu filled with imaginative and unique drink options. The 'Lil Oaty', a drink that's equally refreshing and comforting, is made with pecan macadamia oat milk, espresso, and vegan coconut caramel served with a sprinkle of nutmeg over ice. Just enough sweet with the perfect amount of spice balances the espresso and makes this order great for anyone looking for a deviation from their standard iced latte or dirty chai. Don't miss the other Los Angeles locations, Go Get Em Tiger, in Larchmont Village and Los Feliz.

(213) 265-7718
gandb.coffee

SUN–WED.	7:00am - 7:00pm
THU–SAT.	7:00am - 8:00pm

First opened 2012
Roaster Go Get Em Tiger
Machine La Marzocco Linea PB, 3 groups
Grinder Mazzer Luigi

Espresso	$3.50
Cappuccino	$4.25
Latte	$5.25
Cold brew	$4.50

Sister locations Go Get Em Tiger (Los Feliz) / Go Get Em Tiger (Larchmont)

No. 12

GiorgiPorgi

137 East 3rd Street, CA 90013 | **Little Tokyo**

A successful GiorgiPorgi experience looks like this - you walk in, you take in the stunning atmosphere and you take a seat, waiting for the barista who will come take your order. Don't ask for a menu, there isn't one. Instead, tell the barista what you're in the mood for, and let them make you something you won't easily forget.
The cold brew here is out of this world; smooth with a depth of full bodied flavor you're guaranteed to love. Visiting GiorgiPorgi is an unforgettable experience, from the moss-covered walls to the exceptional brews, as long as you're willing to go with the flow.

giorgiporgi.com

MON-SUN.   8:30am - 4:20pm

First opened 2016
Roaster Multiple roasters
Machine La Marzocco FB70, 3 groups
Grinder Mazzer Luigi Robur

Espresso	$3.00
Cappuccino	$5.00
Latte	$5.00
Cold brew	$5.00

Groundwork Coffee Co. Arts District

811 Traction Avenue, CA 90013 | **Arts District**

Groundwork's Downtown location is almost unrecognizable compared to its more grass-root establishments and is obviously inspired by the creativity and industrial design of the surrounding Arts District. This location is a genuinely pretty place to get work done or meet up with a friend. Baristas are friendly and quick to make your drink and will leave you feeling welcomed and well taken care of. Buying a bag of beans gets you a free cup of delicious coffee, a great way to enjoy Groundwork's excellent coffee at home too. This café has plenty of space and an abundance of tables, so you can comfortably plan to stay a while.

(213) 626-6060
www.groundworkcoffee.com

MON-SUN.   6:00am - 6:00pm

First opened 2015
Roaster Groundwork Coffee Co.
Machine La Marzocco GB5 EE, 2 groups
Grinder Mahlkönig K30 Twin

Espresso	$3.25
Cappuccino	$4.25
Latte	$4.25 / $5.25
Cold brew	$4.50

Sister locations Multiple locations

LOIT Cafe

301 West Olympic Boulevard, CA 90015 | **DTLA**

Photo: Max Milla

LOIT is the freelance worker or student's dream - tons of natural light, long communal tables with built in outlets, and lots of fun and different ways to get caffeinated are all great aspects of this Downtown café. The signature offerings add charcoal to the drinks, creating black matchas, mochas, and lattes that make for an exciting twist on your favorite craft beverage. This place is truly sleek - the interior design is definitely oriented to the fashion-inclined; black and white marble table tops, grey walls, and modular lighting all show off LOIT's interest in creating a truly pleasant atmosphere for its patrons. Counter Culture beans are on bar, a popular draw for LA natives who are on the hunt for a great cup of coffee.

MON-SAT.	8:00am - 7:00pm
SUN.	9:00am - 7:00pm

First opened 2017
Roaster Counter Culture Coffee
Machine La Marzocco Linea, 4 groups
Grinder Nuova Simonelli Mythos One Clima Pro

Espresso	$3.25
Cappuccino	$4.25
Latte	$4.75
Cold brew	$4.50

(213) 372-5102
www.theloit.com/info/losAngeles

Maru Coffee Arts District

1019 South Santa Fe Avenue, CA 90021 | **Arts District**

Massive, open, and chic - Maru's newest location outdoes itself with its minimalist design and total commitment to providing the finest coffees available from multiple roasters. Walking into the shop feels like walking into a day spa - it's quiet, tranquil, and you'll leave feeling at peace. The space is open and bright with exposed beams and a minimalist, industrial feel. The color palette is awash with muted whites and creams, with the stunning Slayer machine and their multiple grinders standing bright white on the bar. Maru collaborates with multiple roasters to craft its beverages, the roasts for pour overs, drip and espresso all staying on rotation. Maru also has plans to roast and serve its own coffee by winter. The baristas are well-trained and know how to bring out the best flavors of each bean. If you're not sure what to order, ask for a recommendation. The baristas know their ever-evolving menu best and are sure to help you find something you'll love.

MON-FRI. 7:00am - 5:00pm
SAT-SUN. 8:00am - 6:00pm

First opened 2018
Roaster Multiple roasters
Machine Slayer Steam X, 3 groups
Grinder Mahlkönig EK 43,
Nuova Simonelli Mythos II

Espresso $3.50
Cappuccino $4.00
Latte $4.50
Cold brew $4.50

(213) 372-5755
marucoffee.com

Sister locations Los Feliz

DTLA & Chinatown

Nice Coffee

555 South Flower Street, CA 90071 | **DTLA**

TOP 40

Photo: Gensler

Nestled in the middle of the grandiose City National Plaza sits the picturesque Nice Coffee, a sweet box-shaped shop filled with delicious drinks and a fabulously cohesive barista team. 49th Parallel Coffee is the roaster of choice, and the three-group La Marzocco machine does a supreme job of bringing out the very best in each espresso pull. The menu is simple and classic - the regulars here are business executives who value a quick, familiar, and reliable coffee break. Grab a light and creamy nitro cold brew for something refreshing, one of the most popular items on the menu.

The plaza is a beautiful place to enjoy your craft coffee, and you'll definitely leave wanting more. Nice job!

www.nicecoffee.com

MON-FRI. 7:00am - 4:00pm
SAT-SUN. Closed

First opened 2017
Roaster 49th Parallel Coffee Roasters
Machine La Marzocco Strada, 3 groups
Grinder Mazzer Luigi Major E

Espresso	$3.25
Cappuccino	$4.00
Latte	$4.50
Cold brew	$4.00

No Ghost Bears

805 East 8th Street, CA 90014 | **DTLA**

Formerly known as Coffee CoLab, No Ghost Bears has stepped up its game with a fresh face - spunky and provocative design elements have elevated this neighborhood favorite. Walking up to the coffee shop you'll probably notice a large group gathered outside interacting, showcasing the shop as a local hub for hanging out. The white La Marzocco espresso machine is decked out in black anime-inspired design, and the black vinyl lettering on the walls spells out cheeky messages to the customers. Ordering the cold brew with a splash of almond milk is a delicious choice, but if you're looking for something sweeter the mocha is a stellar option. If you're interested in making your next coffee run memorable, look no further than this unique DTLA café.

MON-FRI. 7:00am - 6:00pm
SAT-SUN. 8:00am - 5:00pm

First opened 2014
Roaster Suits & Knives
Machine La Marzocco FB80
Grinder Mazzer Luigi

Espresso	$3.00
Cappuccino	$4.00
Latte	$4.75
Cold brew	$5.00

noghostbears.com

The NoMad Los Angeles Coffee Bar

649 South Olive Street, CA 90014 | **DTLA**

In true hotelier fashion, The NoMad Hotel's Coffee Bar continues the venue's obvious commitment to quality and luxury with their combined cocktail and coffee bar. Colombia-to-Brooklyn-based Devoción is the roaster of choice, the honey blend delivering a unique flavor profile of citrus and mild sweetness to every milk-based drink. The coffee cocktails are particularly of note, alcoholic masterpieces that either feature cold brew or a coffee infused dry vermouth. The Sour is a beautiful mix of various liquors and well-balanced cold brew, similar to a whiskey sour but with a beautiful caffeine kick. Quality is the name of the game in this special location, and it's yours to enjoy next time you visit The NoMad Hotel.

(213) 358-0000
www.thenomadhotel.com/los-angeles/dining/coffee-bar

MON-SUN. 6:30am - 3:00pm

First opened 2018
Roaster Devoción
Machine La Marzocco FB80 EE, 2 groups
Grinder Mazzer Luigi Super Jolly E

Espresso	$4.00
Cappuccino	$6.00
Latte	$6.00
Cold brew	$6.00

Nossa Familia Espresso Bar
at The CalEdison DTLA 200 Broadway, CA 90071 | DTLA

A small and simple coffee bar in an enchanting and grandiose space, Nossa Familia brings some craft coffee magic to the lobby of Downtown LA's CalEdison building. This Brazilian-inspired coffee kiosk serves all the traditional espresso-based drinks along with a few other non-coffee customer favorites, such as the popular Brazilian soft drinks Guarana and fresh coconut water. The gleaming white, two-group La Marzocco makes a mean espresso shot and does a great job of providing a base for all of the espresso options. If you're perusing Downtown LA and need to stop for delicious craft coffee, this is a beautiful place to try.

(213) 675-0102
www.nossacoffee.com

MON-FRI. 7:30am - 3:30pm
SAT-SUN. Closed

First opened 2017
Roaster Nossa Familia Coffee
Machine La Marzocco Strada, 2 groups
Grinder Mazzer Luigi Kony

Espresso	$3.00
Cappuccino	$4.00
Latte	$4.00

Paramount Coffee Project DTLA

TOP 10

1320 East 7th Street #100, CA 90021 | **DTLA**

In pursuit of a larger space to roast its own coffee and provide for its fast-growing fan base, Paramount Coffee Project, or PCP, opened this impressive new flagship in The ROW Downtown Los Angeles. Paramount was started by three partners in Sydney, Australia in 2013 with the goal of bringing their own unique vision to their local coffee scene. PCP's Aussie influence is apparent in both the shop's sleek design, as well as its mission to create a relaxed environment for its patrons to enjoy their flavorful espresso. The baristas are engaging and are eager to provide an educational experience to interested customers. This is absolutely a must-visit shop for any discerning LA coffee lover.

(213) 372-5305
pcpdtla.com

MON–SUN.   8:00am – 5:00pm

First opened 2018
Roaster Parlor Coffee Roasters, Neat Coffee, Slate Coffee Roasters, Hidden House Coffee and guests
Machine La Marzocco Linea PB, 3 groups
Grinder Mahlkönig EK 43, Mazzer Luigi Robur

Espresso	$3.50
Cappuccino	$3.50
Latte	$4.00
Cold brew	$5.00

Sister locations Fairfax

RVCC Intersect

2406 East 8th Street, CA 90021 | **DTLA**

Intersect is named after the physical attributes of the shop - there's a connected barber shop and gallery, but it's also inspired by the goal of the owners to be a place for people to intersect. The space is wonderfully moody and well-designed with a long bar, comfortable seating and plenty of wall outlets. If you're a regular of Intersect, you can keep your own mug here to make your morning coffee more comfortable and familiar. The nitro cold brew is smooth and delicate, fruity notes popping in a few seconds after your first sip. You can't go wrong with a classic cappuccino, and the baristas are sure to give you a stellar recommendation if you're unsure of which of their various menu items will suit your preferences.

www.rvccintersect.com

MON-FRI.	7:00am - 7:00pm
SAT-SUN.	8:00am - 7:00pm

First opened 2017
Roaster Tectonic Coffee Co.
Machine Mavam, 2 groups
Grinder Mahlkönig Peak, Mahlkönig EK 43

Espresso	$3.50
Cappuccino	$4.00
Latte	$4.75
Cold brew	$5.00

Spring for Coffee

548 Spring Street #106, CA 90013 | **DTLA**

This shop is one of Downtown's originals, operating on Spring Street, ten years strong and holding its own as a friendly neighborhood shop in the middle of Downtown's hustle and bustle. The cold brew is excellent; an Ethiopian roast from Coava Roasters, creates a perfect balance of fruity, full-bodied, and semi-sweet. The baristas are laid back and super friendly, making you feel welcome from the moment you walk in. If you're in the neighborhood, this wonderful shop deserves a visit.

(213) 228-0041

MON–FRI.	6:30am – 7:30pm
SAT.	7:00am – 7:30pm
SUN.	7:30am – 7:30pm

First opened 2011
Roaster Multiple roasters
Machine La Marzocco GB5, 2 groups
Grinder Ditting

Espresso	$3.50
Cappuccino	$4.00
Latte	$4.00
Cold brew	$4.00

Stumptown Coffee Roasters

806 Santa Fe Avenue, CA 90021 | **DTLA**

Amidst the Arts District vibe of exposed brick and renovated warehouses sits Stumptown Coffee's Los Angeles location - an impressive industrial-style building with lots of Pacific Northwest charm characteristic of this Portland-based brand. Big windows inside of the shop reveal the impressive roastery housed in this location, serving to showcase Stumptown's massive local coffee roasting operation. The espresso blend delivers balanced flavors of cherry, chocolate, and a smooth caramel finish. Baristas are welcoming and knowledgeable, the coffee offerings are numerous, and weekly tastings are available to the public. Stumptown's signature nitro cold brew is available on tap, a refreshing option for the warm Southern California weather. What's not to like about this Stumptown location?

(855) 711-3385
www.stumptowncoffee.com

MON-SUN. 6:30am - 7:00pm

First opened 2013
Roaster Stumptown Coffee Roasters
Machine La Marzocco Strada MP, 3 groups
Grinder Mazzer Luigi x2, Ditting

Espresso	$3.00
Cappuccino	$4.00
Latte	$4.00
Cold brew	$3.75 / $4.75

Tilt Coffee Bar

334 South Main Street #1, CA 90013 | **DTLA**

Moments away from the buzz of the Downtown LA streets is Tilt, a uniquely designed coffee local, hidden away off South Main Street. Featuring three walls of windows, the shop is named for the architecture, as the building appears to be tilted. The owner is a designer, so thoughtful design details are everywhere - a bright and calming color palette, beautiful wood counters and exposed concrete really make this space unlike any other. The cloud latte is out of this world - a lightly sweet, deeply rich latte you'll love if you enjoy sweeter coffee beverages. The baristas here are knowledgeable and know how to extract the best flavors from their delicious beans from Heart Roasters.

www.tiltcoffeebar.com

MON-SAT.	7:00am - 7:00pm
SUN.	9:00am - 6:00pm

First opened 2016
Roaster Heart Coffee Roasters
Machine Synesso MVP Hydra, 2 groups
Grinder Nuova Simonelli Mythos One Clima Pro, Mahlkönig EK 43

Espresso	$3.00
Cappuccino	$4.00
Latte	$4.50
Cold brew	$4.50

Two Guns Espresso

601 South Figueroa Street, CA 90017 | **DTLA**

Located in the heart of Downtown LA's Financial District is Two Guns Espresso, an outdoor café space catering to busy business professionals in need of their daily caffeine fix. Two Guns goes above and beyond its customers' needs with high-quality, house-roasted beans that bring excellent flavor to the drink offerings. A double shot of Two Guns' espresso is a popular order among the regulars of this establishment, with nutty and caramel flavors coming through beautifully in the taste and aroma. If you're looking for a quick coffee to drink as you enjoy the beautiful weather outside, Two Guns is the place to find it.

www.twogunsespresso.com

Sister locations Manhattan Beach / El Segundo

MON-FRI.	7:00am - 4:30pm
SAT-SUN.	Closed

First opened 2015
Roaster Two Guns Espresso
Machine La Marzocco Linea, 2 groups
Grinder Mazzer Luigi Major E

Espresso	$3.00
Cappuccino	$4.00
Latte	$4.55
Cold brew	$4.60

Verve Coffee Roasters Spring Street

833 South Spring Street, CA 90014 | **DTLA**

Verve Coffee Roasters' Los Angeles flagship location is truly magnificent. The floor-to-ceiling outdoor topiary mixed with industrial-style interior design does a great job of representing the heart of Downtown LA - greenery amongst innovation. The espresso is always on point here, and you can't go wrong with any coffee made on the imposing Kees van der Westen. Make sure whatever espresso drink you get is paired with one of the delicious pastries, the croissants are especially of note. If you're looking for a spectacular and unique Los Angeles coffee experience, Verve's Downtown location is just right for you.

(213) 455-5991
www.vervecoffee.com

Sister locations Melrose Avenue / 3rd Street

MON-SUN.   7:00am - 7:00pm

First opened 2015
Roaster Verve Coffee Roasters
Machine Kees van der Westen Spirit, 4 groups
Grinder Nuova Simonelli Mythos, Mahlkönig EK 43

Espresso	$3.00
Cappuccino	$4.00
Latte	$4.75
Cold brew	$4.00

PROFESSIONAL
GUIDE
TO STEAMING
for everyone

1 *Keep It Cool!*
Pour chilled, keep steam temperature lower than milk *(à la cappuccino)*.

2 **While stretching you should hear** *a whisper.*

3 **After 3-5 seconds, tip pitcher to side to begin** *whirlpool.*

Chat with @CalifiaFarms (f) (o)
www.califiafarms.com | sales@califiafarms.com

Midtown & Koreatown

Alchemist Coffee Project

698 South Vermont Avenue #103, CA 90005 | **Koreatown**

Alchemist Coffee Project brings complete care and consideration to the Koreatown coffee scene, with its thoughtfully selected seasonal food and coffee menus. The shop is designed with a French industrial influence, the result of its partnership with a local French designer. Enjoy a Hario pour over with beans from Heart Roasters, one of the numerous brewing methods used here, and receive a truly delectable cup every time. Owner Kim wanted to create a place that fosters diversity and makes everybody that enters feel comfortable and welcome, and you'll find just that when you visit Alchemist.

(213) 388-8767
alchemist-coffee-project.cafes-city.com

MON-SAT.	7:30am -10:00pm
SUN.	8:00am - 10:00pm

First opened 2010
Roaster Heart Coffee Roasters, 49th Parallel Coffee Roasters, Copa Vida Coffee
Machine Synesso Cyncra, 2 groups
Grinder Mahlkönig EK 43

Espresso	$3.00
Cappuccino	$4.00
Latte	$4.50
Cold brew	$4.00

Alfred Coffee Melrose Place

8428 Melrose Place, CA 90069 | **Melrose**

Late afternoon at this iconic Melrose Place coffee shop casts a golden glow on its patio, making it reminiscent of a classic Parisian café. The design inside is so on brand that you'd know you had walked into an Alfred store even without their slogan, 'But First, Coffee', stencilled on the wall. Sit and relax in the plentiful outdoor seating and enjoy your beautiful surroundings. Step into the shop and smell the aroma of Stumptown's fresh beans, excellently prepared by the skilled Alfred baristas. The iced espresso drinks go great with LA's frequently warm weather, and the pastries are particularly notable; especially the matcha dipped croissants. Want something a little special? The Alfred Cone is an espresso or macchiato served in an edible chocolate waffle cone - coffee and a desert rolled into one! When you visit, be sure to grab a bag of Stumptown's custom roast made just for Alfred - it makes a great pour over for that 'first coffee' in the morning.

MON-SUN.   7:00am - 8:00pm

First opened 2013
Roaster Stumptown Coffee Roasters
Machine La Marzocco Linea PB, 4 groups
Grinder Mazzer Luigi Kold E

Espresso	$3.00
Cappuccino	$4.00
Latte	$4.50
Cold brew	$4.00

(323) 944-0811
alfred.la

Sister locations Multiple locations

Midtown & Koreatown

Alibi Coffee Co.

2268 Venice Boulevard, CA 90006 | **Harvard Heights**

Alibi is a hidden gem bordering Koreatown and Historic West Adams - a lovely addition to the local coffee scene. This roastery and coffee shop combo makes a mean cup of coffee, and the entire front of the shop is devoted to a large pool table. Alibi is classy but has a definite quirky side and isn't afraid to show it. It offers $1.50 drip all day, which means your quality coffee run will also be affordable. Grab your favorite coffee order and relax - this is a place you'll love to spend your time.

www.alibicoffeecompany.com

MON-SUN. 8:00am - 3:00pm

First opened 2017
Roaster Alibi Coffee Co.
Machine La Marzocco FB80, 3 groups
Grinder Mazzer Luigi Kony

Espresso	$2.50
Cappuccino	$3.75
Latte	$4.00
Cold brew	$4.50

Bluestone Lane La Brea

76 South La Brea Avenue, CA 90036 | **Hancock Park**

Bluestone Lane on La Brea is wonderfully enchanting. The expertly designed interior creates a pleasing, peaceful environment to enjoy your morning cup. Everything you order will be deliciously and aesthetically prepared, and all items on the food menu can be made gluten free. A single origin espresso is a great choice, as is its famous flat white. Bluestone Lane has its espresso protocol down to a science, however an Aussie iced latte is another sweet option worth considering from the extensive menu.

(718) 374-6858
bluestonelane.com

Sister locations Studio City /
Santa Monica / Venice

MON-SUN.   7:30am - 7:00pm

First opened 2018
Roaster Bluestone Lane Coffee
Machine La Marzocco Linea PB, 2 groups
Grinder Mazzer Luigi Super Jolly

Espresso	$3.00
Cappuccino	$4.25
Latte	$4.25
Cold brew	$4.00

Coffee For Sasquatch

70 Melrose Avenue, CA 90038 | **Melrose**

Coffee For Sasquatch is the definition of slick. Minimalist design defines this West Hollywood shop. And true to its name, a giant sasquatch can be spotted creeping across the wall, framed with gleaming silver and luscious greenery. Order a cryptid latte, a stunning array of colors incorporated into a classic latte, for something bright and very special.

For something more understated, but just as tasty, the honey cardamom latte will not disappoint. But to really appreciate the fragrant beans, go for a light and flavorful pour over. Ritual coffee is what's on bar, and with a rotating menu of blends, Coffee For Sasquatch keeps its espresso options current and fresh. Plenty of indoor seating, electrical outlets, and free WiFi make

this an incredible workspace. Coffee For Sasquatch is picture perfect without people, so count yourself lucky if you ever find you have this highly popular spot to yourself.

MON–SAT. 7:00am – 7:00pm
SUN. 7:00am – 6:00pm

First opened 2017
Roaster Ritual Coffee Roasters
Machine La Marzocco Strada, 3 groups
Grinder Mahlkönig EK 43,
Mazzer Luigi Robur E

Espresso $3.25
Cappuccino $4.00
Latte $4.75
Cold brew $5.00

(323) 424-7980
coffeeforsasquatch.com

Midtown & Koreatown

Document Coffee Bar

3850 Wilshire Boulevard, CA 90010 | **Koreatown**

This Koreatown gem was once a well-known art gallery, so artist co-owners Sojung Kwon and Byoungok Koh went to work to create something meaningful in the space, reviving it with sleek minimalist design and delicious coffee. The well-rounded coffee menu features the classics as well as some imaginative options like the Document Latte, a traditional latte sweetened with maple syrup. Document also touts an impressive tea menu with almost every option available, many sourced directly from Korea. Stumptown's Hairbender single-origin is the bedrock of the espresso options and pour over coffees are kept fresh and new by frequently rotating the menu and serving beans from up and coming roasters. If you're looking for a good workspace and great coffee, Document is a sound bet.

(310) 465-8135
documentcoffeebar.com

MON–SUN. 7:00am – 7:00pm

First opened 2014
Roaster Multiple roasters
Machine La Marzocco Linea EE, 3 groups
Grinder Mahlkönig EK 43, Compak F10, Versalab M3

Espresso	$3.25
Cappuccino	$4.50
Latte	$4.75
Cold brew	$5.00

Go Get Em Tiger Larchmont

230 North Larchmont Boulevard, CA 90004 | **Hancock Park**

The Larchmont Village location of Go Get Em Tiger is frequently abuzz with activity. It's a highly popular spot to get good food as well as high-end specialty coffee, with menu items like avocado toast and house smoked salmon tartine serving as tremendously popular options. First and foremost, however, Go Get Em Tiger is a craft coffee shop - the espresso stands out for its consistently smooth and rich flavor. The shop itself is beautiful, with clean design and a warm atmosphere. Go Get Em makes its own almond macadamia milk in house, which tastes creamy with a hint of tang in a latte. With a menu and service this good, Go Get Em has easily established itself as a cut above most in the sparkling Los Angeles coffee scene.

(323) 380-5359
gget.la

MON-SUN. 6:30am - 6:00pm

First opened 2013
Roaster Go Get Em Tiger
Machine La Marzocco Linea PB, 3 groups
Grinder Mazzer Luigi

Espresso	$3.50
Cappuccino	$4.25
Latte	$5.25
Cold brew	$4.50

Sister locations Loz Feliz / G&B (DTLA)

LaB Coffee & Roasters

429 North Western Avenue #5, CA 90004 | **Koreatown**

Boasting an impressive number of brewing methods, LaB Coffee Roasters lives up to its name by making its customer's coffee experience one of variety to fit any kind of coffee preference. Numerous single origin and milk-based espresso options make it easy to find something that you'll enjoy. Electrical outlets and seating are plentiful, making this a phenomenal workspace. Try a Costa Rican pour over if you're in the mood for a sip-by-sip experience akin to curling up with a good book, or grab their 'Mad For Caffeine' option to try three different origins of coffees, all served creatively in chemistry-inspired dishware.

(323) 465-6788
labcoffee.com

MON-FRI.	7:30am - 9:00pm
SAT-SUN.	8:30am - 9:00pm

First opened 2015
Roaster LaB Coffee & Roasters
Machine Victoria Arduino Black Eagle, 2 groups
Grinder Mahlkönig EK 43

Espresso	$3.50
Cappuccino	$4.50
Latte	$5.00
Cold brew	$4.00

Paramount Coffee Project Fairfax

456 North Fairfax Avenue, CA 90036 | **Fairfax**

This Aussie-born brand Paramount Coffee Project, aka PCP, really gives itself away with its trendy design, imaginative food menu, and superb espresso options. The coffee is rich and flavorful, and ultimately the result of the shop's commitment to blind tastings - every roaster Paramount features is selected purely based on taste. Integrity is the name of the game, and you see it in every aspect of the shop. Every barista is beyond friendly and is sure to make your favorite espresso drink exactly to your liking. Paramount Coffee Project stands out for its extraordinary quality and poise in food, coffee, atmosphere and service. One not to be missed.

(323) 746-5480
pcpfx.com

Sister locations DTLA

| MON-SAT. | 7:00am - 5:00pm |
| SUN. | 8:00am - 5:00pm |

First opened 2015
Roaster Sweet Bloom Coffee Roasters, Sey Coffee, Slate Coffee Roasters, Heart Coffee Roasters, Case Coffee Roasters and guests
Machine La Marzocco Linea PB
Grinder Mahlkönig EK 43, Mazzer Luigi Kold

Espresso	$3.50
Cappuccino	$4.00
Latte	$4.00
Cold brew	$4.00

Point Five

7965 1/2 Melrose Avenue, CA 90046 | **Melrose**

This Hollywood gem is cute, chic and provides excellent coffee. Espressos here rotate, so ask the barista for a drink recommendation to try the best of whatever is on bar. The roast comes through amazingly in the flat white and you will also be amazed by the quality of the latte art. Point Five is all about making everything in the shop contribute to a truly happy experience for customers.
The interior is sleek, yet comfortable. The double chocolate mocha is a nice sweeter option that showcases the espresso really well. The matcha smoothie also deserves a mention.

(323) 424-7723
www.pointfiveespressobar.com

MON-SAT.	7:00am – 6:00pm
SUN.	8:00am – 6:00pm

First opened 2018
Roaster Common Room Roasters
Machine La Marzocco Linea PB ABR, 3 groups
Grinder Mazzer Luigi Kony E

Espresso	$3.50
Cappuccino	$4.25
Latte	$4.50
Cold brew	$5.00

République

624 South La Brea Avenue, CA 90036 | **Hancock Park**

This enchanting space makes it seem as though a mythical castle was dropped in the middle of Los Angeles. It has a gothic feel, and the line out the door shows how popular it is. The atmosphere is engaging and comfortable, and it's obvious that this place is intended to feel luxurious. The food options are plentiful, but this establishment really stands out with its coffee - made with a full-bodied roast that pairs well with anything else you may feel inclined to order. If you're looking for a well-rounded experience, République will make your day.

(310) 362-6115
www.republiquela.com

MON-SUN.   8:00am - 3:00pm

First opened 2013
Roaster LAMILL Coffee,
Verve Coffee Roasters
Machine La Marzocco Linea, 3 groups
Grinder Mahlkönig Guatemala

Espresso	$3.50
Cappuccino	$4.50
Latte	$5.00
Cold brew	$5.00

second round cafe

207 North Western Avenue, CA 90004 | **Koreatown**

second round is named for the Korean bar scene, referring to a second round of drinks. Co-owners Jeff and James' vision for their café was to create a bar-inspired shop open late to accommodate Koreatown night owls. Moody lighting and contrasting black and white walls emulate a definite nightlife feel. second round keeps with its bar theme by offering various coffee and tea options on tap, as well as offering expertly crafted pour overs.

(323) 327-2824
secondround.github.io

SUN-THU.	10:30am - 12:00am
FRI-SAT.	10:30am - 2:00am

First opened 2018
Roaster Stumptown Coffee Roasters, Stereoscope Coffee Co, Cognoscenti Coffee, Elim Coffee Roasters
Grinder Bunn G1

Cold brew $5.50

spl. coffee

4059 West 3rd Street, CA 90020 | **Koreatown**

spl. (pronounced 'spill', short for 'spill the beans') is a casual and comfortable environment great for visiting with friends or getting work done. spl.'s mission is to make specialty coffee accessible to anyone who enjoys a good cup by keeping this tidy environment very relaxed and laid back. The espresso is smooth and buttery, produced and roasted by LA local roastery Lightwave, and pairs beautifully with milk. The co-owner always dreamed of opening a coffee shop as a child, and has realized her dream with this intimate, modern addition to the fast-growing Koreatown coffee scene.

(213) 915-0037

MON-FRI.	7:00am - 8:00pm
SAT-SUN.	8:00am - 8:00pm

First opened 2017
Roaster Lightwave Coffee Roasters
Machine La Marzocco Linea, 2 groups
Grinder Mahlkönig Peak, Mazzer Luigi

Espresso	$3.00
Cappuccino	$3.75
Latte	$4.50
Cold brew	$3.75

Verve Coffee Roasters 3rd Street

8051 West 3rd Street, CA 90048 | **Beverly Grove**

This sprawling shop does many things well. The layout is aesthetic, open, and comfortable, with plenty of seating and the occasional wall outlet giving you the option to settle in and get work done here. The gleaming four-group Kees van der Westen sits atop the stunning horseshoe shaped bar, so opt for an espresso drink to see this beautiful machine in its full glory. Verve has its roasts dialled in to a tee, making the espresso consistently tasty and smooth. If you're feeling like something a little lighter, one of the fragrant pour overs will be sure to hit the spot. The baristas are friendly and skilled, so order anything that suits your fancy and end up with an expertly crafted beverage kindly delivered. Can't get enough of this great coffee? Pick up a bag of Verve's own beans and some brewing equipment and recreate your favorite drinks at home. Great service, delicious coffee and a beautifully inviting space makes this a great place to stop for your favorite coffee order.

MON–SUN.   7:00am – 8:00pm

First opened 2015
Roaster Verve Coffee Roasters
Machine Kees van der Westen Spirit,
4 groups
Grinder Nuova Simonelli Mythos x3,
Mahlkönig EK 43

Espresso	$3.00
Cappuccino	$4.00
Latte	$4.75
Cold brew	$4.00

(323) 424-7008
www.vervecoffee.com

Sister locations Melrose Avenue /
Spring Street

Midtown & Koreatown

Silver Lake, Echo Park & Los Feliz

Alfred Coffee Silver Lake

3337 1/2 Sunset Boulevard, CA 90026 | **Silver Lake**

Bold design and the infamous slogan, 'But First, Coffee', makes Alfred Silver Lake instantly recognizable. The walls, as well as being adorned with the neon slogan, are decorated with vibrant floral wallpaper and beautiful gold plant transfers. Stumptown espresso pulled on a three-group La Marzocco ensures a consistently delicious cup every time, with or without silky milk and stunning latte art. Bored of having your coffee in a regular cup? Have it in The Alfred Cone instead! (A waffle cone filled with espresso or macchiato.) Order the signature $10 latte if you want to be adventurous; a latte with additions like Pressed Juiceries almond milk and extra espresso shots that make it well worth the upcharge. Meal time or not, pair your coffee with a bagel

for a perfectly rounded experience. With vibrant design, an open patio, and Alfred's signature coffee offerings, Alfred stands in Los Angeles as a community favorite.

MON-FRI.	6:30am - 5:00pm
SAT-SUN.	7:30am - 6:00pm

First opened 2015
Roaster Stumptown Coffee Roasters
Machine La Marzocco GB5, 3 groups
Grinder Mazzer Luigi Kony E

Espresso	$3.00
Cappuccino	$4.00
Latte	$4.50
Cold brew	$4.00

(323) 522-6984
alfred.la

Sister locations Multiple locations

Silver Lake, Echo Park & Los Feliz

Andante Coffee Roasters

2201 West Sunset Boulevard, CA 90026 | **Echo Park**

Make your way to Andante Coffee Roasters in Silver Lake for your morning coffee run and be greeted by friendly baristas who will make you a lovely cup to start your day with. This cozy shop makes a great hang out, and with espresso this good, you may have trouble leaving. The consistency and quality of the coffee is superb, as is the beautiful latte art. Order an Ethiopian pour over to make the most of the fruity, milk-chocolate notes. Andante Coffee, always worth the visit.

(213) 568-3099

Sister locations Fairfax / DTLA

MON-SAT.	7:30am - 7:00pm
SUN.	8:30am - 7:00pm

First opened 2014
Roaster Andante Coffee Roasters
Machine La Marzocco Linea PB, 3 groups
Grinder Mahlkönig EK 43,
Mazzer Luigi Kold

Espresso	$3.00
Cappuccino	$4.00
Latte	$4.00
Cold brew	$3.75

Bru Coffeebar

1866 North Vermont Avenue, CA 90027 | **Los Feliz**

Warm and inviting, Bru in Los Feliz is a great spot to find some solace along with your favorite coffee beverage. Cool design and plenty of tables is only part of what makes this shop so appealing; the tasty espresso is the real highlight of this venue. Smooth and delicate, it pairs really well with milk for a delicious latte or get it with hot water for a fulfilling americano. The tea options are plentiful here as well, in case you're looking for a change of pace.

(323) 664-7500
brucoffeebar.com

MON-SUN.   7:00am - 8:00pm

First opened 2011
Roaster Ritual Coffee Roasters
Machine La Marzocco FB80, 3 groups
Grinder Mahlkönig EK 43, Mazzer Luigi Super Jolly, Mazzer Luigi Major E

Espresso	$3.25
Cappuccino	$5.00
Latte	$5.00
Cold brew	$5.00

Caffe Vita Coffee Roasting Co.

4459 Sunset Boulevard, CA 90027 | **Los Feliz**

Originating from Seattle, Caffe Vita's Silver Lake location is often a hub of activity. A popular destination for laptop users and coffee fiends alike, this café's vibe is relaxed and comfortable. It's the perfect place to unwind with a cold brew and a bagel or a classic cappuccino. The shop is situated between Silver Lake and Los Feliz, making it centrally located to the best that both neighborhoods have to offer. If you're looking for a local favorite, Caffe Vita is a great choice.

(323) 663-6340
caffevita.com

MON-FRI.	6:00am - 8:00pm
SAT-SUN.	7:00am - 8:00pm

First opened 2013
Roaster Caffe Vita Coffee Roasting Co.
Machine Kees van der Westen Spirit, 3 groups
Grinder Mazzer Luigi x2

Espresso	$3.25
Cappuccino	$4.25
Latte	$4.50
Cold brew	$4.50

Dayglow

3206 Sunset Boulevard, CA 90026 | **Silver Lake**

Dayglow is fresh and inviting, with an eclectic look and neon accents. It serves multiple well-known roasters, keeping the espresso options updated and on par with excellence. Wide open doors keep the interior space fresh and light, and the friendly baristas are skilled at making you a drink to suit your taste. For a unique twist on a popular favorite, order the military latte, a matcha latte with a shot of espresso thrown in. Dayglow is a no-longer-hidden gem on the Sunset strip, and very deserving of a visit.

(312) 576-6636
dayglow.coffee

MON-SUN.   7:00am - 7:00pm

First opened 2018
Roaster Multiple roasters
Machine La Marzocco Linea PB, 2 groups
Grinder Mahlkönig EK 43, Mahlkönig K30 Air

Espresso	$3.00 / $4.00
Cappuccino	$4.75
Latte	$5.00
Cold brew	$5.00

Dinosaur Coffee

4334 Sunset Boulevard, CA 90029 | **Silver Lake**

Open and airy, Dinosaur Coffee stands out with its striking wooden architecture, but ultimately shines with its friendly service, coffee excellence and laid-back atmosphere. With a rounded-out bar, comfortable outside seating, private tables, as well as a communal table, Dinosaur makes a great place to get work done or gather with friends. Exposed beams, flag stone floor and creative woodwork making up the shelving and menu boards come together with the white walls to create a space that feels simultaneously light and cozy. The espresso stays on rotation throughout the week, ensuring a pleasant variety of flavors for Dinosaur regulars. If you're not sure what to order, try the coconut cold brew, a smooth and slightly sweet twist on an old favorite. Indulge in a delicious baked good while you sip your expertly pulled espresso and relax in the dynamic environment. The shop is full of thoughtful details, from the bright red La Marzocco espresso machine to the occasional plastic dinosaur serving as decor.

MON-SUN. 7:00am - 7:00pm

First opened 2014
Roaster Dogwood Coffee Co.
Machine La Marzocco FB80, 2 groups
Grinder Mazzer Luigi

Espresso	$3.50
Cappuccino	$4.25
Latte	$4.75
Cold brew	$3.75

(330) 502-0046
www.dinosaurcoffee.com

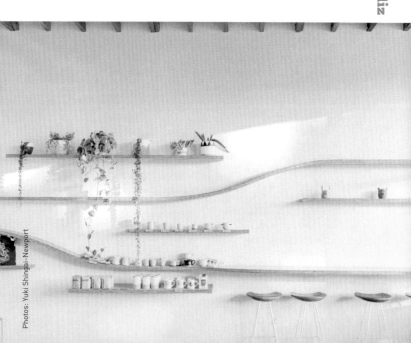

Photos: Yuki Shingai-Newport

Eightfold Coffee

1294 Sunset Boulevard, CA 90026 | **Echo Park**

Sitting picturesque on the edge of Echo Park is Eightfold Coffee, one of the coffee shops that line the Sunset Boulevard promenade. Sunlight pouring through the large windows, plenty of seating, and espresso by Heart Coffee Roasters make this shop a neighborhood treasure.
The space is open and bright, the design is minimal and chic, and a wall of zines showcase this shop's support of local artists. The baristas do an excellent job of bringing out the espresso's chocolatey flavor, and it pairs really well with any of the milk or non-milk options. Grab a classic latte from Eightfold for a fantastic coffee experience.

(213) 947-3500
www.eightfoldcoffee.com

MON–SUN. 7:00am - 6:00pm

First opened 2016
Roaster Heart Coffee Roasters
Machine La Marzocco Linea, 3 groups
Grinder Mahlkönig,
Nuova Simonelli Mythos

Espresso	$3.00
Cappuccino	$4.00
Latte	$4.50
Cold brew	$4.50

Go Get Em Tiger Los Feliz

4630 Hollywood Boulevard, CA 90027 | **Los Feliz**

Go Get Em Tiger, the creation of the renowned Kyle Glanville and Charles Babinski, stands out not only for its good looks and exceptional espresso, but also for its unwavering commitment to quality coffee. Upon entering the shop you'll find the Go Get Em baristas ready to welcome you and share their passion for creating a great cup of coffee. Surrounded by lush greenery and outdoor seating, Go Get Em makes drinking a coffee outside a truly special experience. Bringing a unique twist to traditional espresso orders with a palate-cleansing fizzy hoppy tea, Go Get Em Tiger's ingenuity makes it a true stand-out in an increasingly competitive landscape.

(323) 543-4438
gget.la

MON-SUN. 6:00am - 6:00pm

First opened 2016
Roaster Go Get Em Tiger
Machine La Marzocco Linea PB, 2 groups
Grinder Mazzer Luigi

Espresso	$3.50
Cappuccino	$4.25
Latte	$5.25
Cold brew	$4.50

Sister locations Larchmont / G&B (DTLA)

Intelligentsia Coffee Silver Lake
Coffeebar 3922 Sunset Boulevard, CA 90029 | Silver Lake

This iconic Sunset Boulevard location is hard to miss, often sporting a line out the door and a plethora of seating on the patio. Intelligentsia has become a household name in the coffee industry and lives up to its reputation with expertly roasted coffee beans and skilled baristas who know how to help the beans perform to their full potential. Ordering a latte here will guarantee a lovely cup, and a dirty chai is a great way to kick your normal coffee order up a notch.

(323) 663-6173
www.intelligentsiacoffee.com

Sister locations Venice / Pasadena / Hollywood (coming soon)

SUN-WED.	6:00am - 8:00pm
THU-SAT.	6:00am - 10:00pm

First opened 2007
Roaster Intelligentsia
Machine La Marzocco Linea, 2 groups, La Marzocco Linea PB, 2 groups
Grinder Mahlkönig EK 43, Mazzer Luigi

Espresso	$3.50
Cappuccino	$4.25
Latte	$4.50
Cold brew	$4.50

La Colombe Coffee Roasters

3900 West Sunset Boulevard, CA 90029 | Silver Lake

TOP 40

La Colombe has everything a high-end craft coffee establishment should offer. Its single origin espresso is full bodied and well balanced, all of the coffee options are ethically sourced, and the skilled and friendly baristas help make the well-designed environment feel even more comfortable. Centrally located to Sunset Junction, La Colombe makes a great stop on your way through this highly caffeinated and trendy neighborhood. Order the draft latte for a creamy, delicious coffee on tap. If you're dairy free, order a hemp or oat milk latte, both environmentally friendly alternatives to almond milk.

(323) 375-5370
www.lacolombe.com

Sister locations Century City / Frogtown / Beverly Hills

MON-FRI.	6:30am - 7:00pm
SAT-SUN.	7:00am - 7:00pm

First opened 2017
Roaster La Colombe Coffee Roasters
Machine La Marzocco GB5, 3 groups
Grinder Nuova Simonelli Mythos, Baratza Forté

Espresso	$3.00
Cappuccino	$4.00
Latte	$4.00
Cold brew	$4.00

LAMILL Coffee

1636 Silver Lake Boulevard, CA 90026 | **Silver Lake**

TOP 40

LAMILL stands out with its uniquely stylish food and coffee experience. Classy yet comfortable, the space offers equal opportunity to get work done, visit with friends, or relax with a great coffee in hand. For something sweet, order the orange-infused cappuccino, a balanced and flavorful alternative to an old favorite. An extensive food menu full of lunch options and pastries round out LAMILL as a full-service coffee shop and make it an easy place to spend your afternoon.

(323) 663-4441
lamillcoffee.com

Sister locations Beverly Center / LAX

MON–SUN.   7:00am - 7:00pm

First opened 2008
Roaster LAMILL Coffee
Machine La Marzocco FB80, 3 groups
Grinder Mahlkönig K30, Mazzer Luigi Robur, Ditting

Espresso	$3.00
Cappuccino	$4.00
Latte	$4.25
Cold brew	$3.75

Maru Coffee Los Feliz

1936 Hillhurst Avenue, CA 90027 | **Los Feliz**

A compact venue featuring clean design and plenty of natural sunlight, Maru Coffee in Los Feliz has captured the hearts of the surrounding neighborhood. With patrons from all walks of life, Maru has established itself as an East Side favourite.

The espresso is dark and flavorful and is presented pleasantly in custom designed dishware by Notary Ceramics. Order a macchiato to really taste the exquisite espresso blend. If you're looking for a shop full of thoughtful design details and a variety of coffee options, Maru is a superb choice.

(323) 741-8483
marucoffee.com

Sister locations Arts District

MON-SAT.   7:00am - 6:00pm
SUN.   8:00am - 6:00pm

First opened 2016
Roaster Multiple roasters
Machine Synesso MVP, 2 groups
Grinder Mahlkönig EK 43, Mahlkönig K30, Nuova Simonelli Mythos One

Espresso	$3.50
Cappuccino	$4.00
Latte	$4.50
Cold brew	$4.50

Pollen

2100 Echo Park Avenue, CA 90026 | **Echo Park**

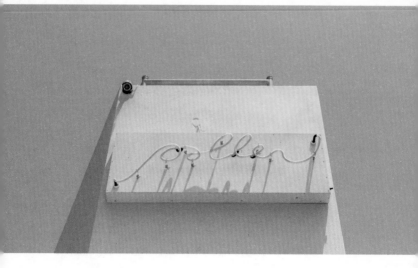

In a beautiful neighborhood in Echo Park sits Pollen, a lovely brunch spot that has its coffee operation down to a science. Tables and chairs are available outside for a sit-down experience, and a tastefully designed espresso bar surrounds the inside of the café if you're looking for a more casual experience. This venue is a real beauty, playing to Southern California's token sunny weather by offering a sheer canopy over the seating, creating coverage from the sun while still allowing the breeze to make its way through the outdoor space as you enjoy your incredible food and coffee. True to its Australian culinary heritage, the flat whites here are especially of note, the milk doing an amazing job of bringing out the flavors in the Jetty espresso. If you want a stellar brunch experience with excellent coffee, make sure to visit Pollen.

| MON–WED. | 8:00am – 3:00pm |
| THU–SUN. | 8:00am – 7:00pm |

First opened 2017
Roaster Jetty Coffee Roasters
Machine La Marzocco GB5, 3 groups
Grinder Mazzer Luigi

Espresso	$2.50
Cappuccino	$4.00 / $4.50
Latte	$4.00 / $4.50
Cold brew	$3.50

(323) 486-7650
www.pollenlosangeles.com

Silver Lake, Echo Park & Los Feliz

Roo Coffee

1523 Griffith Park Boulevard, CA 90026 | **Silver Lake**

Roo is passionate about good coffee and good food. The four Australian owners are friends and bring to Roo what they love most about Australian coffee culture, namely the friendly, hospitable service. Counter Culture espresso is on bar, a balanced and flavorful roaster that serves as Roo's staple coffee supplier. Roo's primary objective is to serve great coffee, and it does this beautifully whilst also creating a welcoming and comfortable environment for its customers. True to form, the shop fosters a laid back and light-hearted atmosphere. Drop by here if you want a coffee experience that leaves you feeling fresh and satisfied.

(818) 879-3890
roouniverse.com

MON–SAT.	7:00am – 5:00pm
SUN.	8:00am – 5:00pm

First opened 2018
Roaster Counter Culture Coffee
Machine La Marzocco Linea PB, 3 groups
Grinder Nuova Simonelli Mythos One Clima Pro

Espresso	$3.50
Cappuccino	$4.50
Latte	$4.50

Scout

3707 Sunset Boulevard, CA 90026 | **Silver Lake**

MON-SUN.   7:00am - 7:00pm

Sandwiched between two popular restaurants under common ownership with Scout, you can expect to find good coffee in addition to delicious pastries and great food for lunch. Scout is primarily a grab and go location. Its goal is to be a one-stop-shop for a dinner party, selling plenty of wine, snacks, and gifts. The espresso from Heart Roasters is consistent and recognizable in flavor and pairs beautifully with the house-made almond milk.

(323) 451-9750
www.scoutsilverlake.com

First opened 2018
Roaster Heart Coffee Roasters
Machine La Marzocco Linea, 2 groups
Grinder Curtis

Espresso	$3.50
Cappuccino	$4.50
Latte	$5.00
Cold brew	$4.50

Starbucks Reserve

2134 Sunset Boulevard, CA 90026 | **Echo Park**

This Starbucks Reserve holds its own in the craft coffee world, and in many ways exceeds its competition with exceptional service, endless drink options, plus regular coffee tastings of rare and unusual coffees. The space itself is imposing and spectacular, hugely high ceilings and two areas to order coffee make this coffee shop especially comfortable. The small-lot Reserve coffees make it easy to enjoy a deliciously smooth single-origin Guatemalan, or a robust Nicaraguan roast, or whatever is newly rotated on bar. Paired with the airy, comfortable atmosphere, you'll find it easy to relax and enjoy your time here.

(213) 431-5969
www.starbucks.com

Sister locations La Brea / Los Feliz

MON-SUN.   5:00am - 10:00pm

First opened 2018
Roaster Starbucks Reserve
Machine Victoria Arduino Black Eagle, 2 groups
Grinder Nuova Simonelli Mythos One x2

Espresso	$3.50
Cappuccino	$4.00
Latte	$4.00
Cold brew	$3.50

Stories Books & Cafe

1716 Sunset Boulevard, CA 90026 | **Echo Park**

There are lots of loveable aspects to Stories Café, with the enchanting bookstore side of the shop rivalling the espresso for first place. Ultimately, however, homage must be paid to all the wonderful drinks offered here. Rather than losing out on quality due to the dual nature of the shop, the opposite seems to be the case - good books and good coffee go hand in hand for this sweet Echo Park hideout. It's open late, too, so it's buzzing with activity well through to the end of the day. You can't go wrong with a classic cappuccino, but a macchiato really brings out the flavors of their Bicycle Coffee espresso. You will enjoy Stories cover to cover.

(213) 413-3733
storiesla.com

SUN-THU.	8:00am - 11:00pm
FRI-SAT.	8:00am - 12:00am

First opened 2008
Roaster Bicycle Coffee Company
Machine La Marzocco Linea
Grinder Mazzer Luigi

Espresso	$3.00
Cappuccino	$3.25
Latte	$3.50
Cold brew	$3.00

TRINITI

1814 Sunset Boulevard, CA 90026 | **Echo Park**

Relationships are the name of the game at Triniti, with every last detail of the shop being the result of a connection made or partnership created. Triniti serves a new guest roaster every month, locally sources the finest produce for its artisanal food options, and even the to-go cups are sourced from a company that makes them out of recycled corn husks. Everything in the shop is thoughtful, and the espresso bar with its sleek Mavam machine is no exception. The black sesame cappuccino is a unique experience, bringing a dark and smoky flavor to the traditional milky espresso. But far from being just a coffee shop, Tritini is a wonderful 'fine casual' LA foodie spot, and one of the best, with chef Joe Geiskopf's fresh and innovative culinary talents on show alongside the perfect coffee offer.

MON-SUN. 8:00am - 5:00pm

First opened 2017
Roaster Coffee Manufactory and guests
Machine Mavam, 2 groups
Grinder Nuova Simonelli Mythos One

Espresso	$4.00
Cappuccino	$4.25
Latte	$4.50
Cold brew	$5.00

(213) 822-2103
www.triniti.la

WKNDR

1820 North Vermont Avenue, CA 90027 | **Los Feliz**

A rotating menu of creative drink options and plenty of bar seating showcase WKNDR's unique bar-style set up, the result of the owner's interest in creating an artisanal coffee experience for his patrons. The espresso from San Francisco-based Sightglass is perfectly showcased in the rotating menu, providing a nutty, dark chocolatey flavor base to the milk drink options. The cold brew is smooth and delicious and is often available paired with other great flavors like sea salt, caramel, or whiskey. The menu changes often to accommodate new and interesting flavor experiences, so have one of the WKNDR baristas make you an expert recommendation.

(323) 922-6032
wkndr.cafe

MON-SUN.   7:00am - 7:00pm

First opened 2018
Roaster Sightglass Coffee
Machine La Marzocco Strada, 3 groups
Grinder Fiorenzato F64 EVO

Espresso	$3.50
Cappuccino	$4.00
Latte	$4.50
Cold brew	$4.00

Sister locations Bardonna (Brentwood / Santa Monica / Larchmont Village / DTLA)

Woodcat Coffee Bar

1532 Sunset Boulevard, CA 90026 | **Echo Park**

The first thing you'll notice entering Woodcat Coffee is the accented red wall and kitschy design, the result of Woodcat's owners Saadat and Janine Awan's hand in designing this unique and comfortable space in which to serve their coffee. The shop's brewing parameters are strictly adhered to, guaranteeing a consistently delicious coffee experience for all its patrons. Flat whites are done right by Woodcat's expert baristas, delivering a smooth, delicious cup that will make you eager to order here again and again.

(213) 537-0147
www.woodcatcoffee.com

MON-FRI.   6:00am - 6:00pm
SAT-SUN.   7:00am - 6:00pm

First opened 2014
Roaster Flat Track Coffee
Machine Faema E61 Legend, 3 groups
Grinder Mahlkönig,
Nuova Simonelli Mythos One

Espresso	$3.00
Cappuccino	$4.00
Latte	$4.50

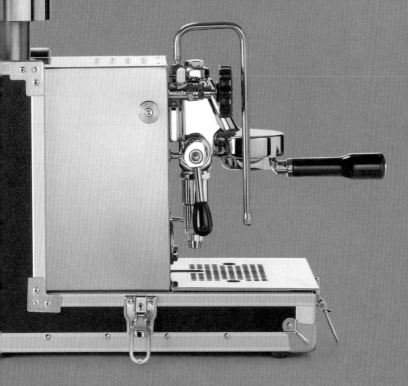

PORTA VIA

The Porta Via is the world's first truly portable espresso machine allowing people to enjoy the Rocket Espresso experience where ever they are.

Travel just got a whole lot more interesting – that 3 star hotel just went to a 5 star.

West Hollywood
& Hollywood

The Assembly

634 North Robertson Boulevard, CA 90069 | **West Hollywood**

The Assembly's aesthetic is clean and minimal, and the menu is imaginative and exciting. The shop was designed to be a place for the community, and this goal is made evident by all the regulars that come through the shop. Plenty of outdoor seating and a thoughtfully curated selection of lifestyle items and stationary make this a unique Hollywood coffee spot. Counter Culture espresso is on bar and tastes especially great in a macchiato. Check out the daily menu for the pour overs as The Assembly regularly rotates its offerings to keep it Hollywood fresh.

(424) 245-4954
theassemblycafe.com

MON-FRI.	7:00am - 6:00pm
SAT.	8:00am - 5:00pm
SUN.	8:00am -3:00pm

First opened 2015
Roaster Counter Culture Coffee
Machine La Marzocco Linea PB, 2 groups
Grinder Mahlkönig EK 43, Mazzer Luigi Robur, Mazzer Luigi Kony

Espresso	$3.25
Cappuccino	$4.25
Latte	$4.75
Cold brew	$5.00

Blackwood Coffee Bar

7509 Sunset Boulevard, CA 90046 | **Hollywood**

Blackwood Coffee Bar is a classy addition to the Hollywood coffee scene, with stunning green tiles behind the counter, a beautiful wood and marble bar, and a posh outdoor patio. The coffee is robust, velvety, and reliably delicious. The Latin cold brew is a fun menu option; cold brew coffee mixed with cashew horchata and Aztec chocolate bitters which makes for a uniquely delicious order. The staff are kind and knowledgeable and are sure to make your experience a truly memorable one.

(323) 848-4217
www.blackwoodcoffeebar.com

MON-FRI.	7:00am - 5:00pm
SAT.	7:00am - 4:00pm
SUN.	8:00am - 4:00pm

First opened 2016
Roaster Caffe Luxxe, Rose Park Roasters
Machine La Marzocco GB5, 2 groups
Grinder Mazzer Luigi Super Jolly

Espresso	$3.50
Cappuccino	$4.50
Latte	$4.75
Cold brew	$4.50

Bluestone Lane Studio City

12186 Ventura Boulevard, CA 91604 | **Silver Triangle**

Paradisiacal, whimsical, and sleek - just a few words to describe Bluestone Lane's Studio City shop. The architecture of the shop stands out for its modular shape and industrial feel. Looking for a coffee that will blow your mind? Look no further than Bluestone's tried and true espresso options. You can't go wrong with an iced latte, and for the true coffee fanatic, a long black with a single origin espresso shot is a delectable choice. Bring a friend with you; you'll both want to gush over the spectacular food, coffee, and hospitable service you'll receive here.

(718) 374-6858
www.bluestonelane.com

Sister locations La Brea / Venice / Santa Monica

MON–SUN. 7:00am – 6:00pm

First opened 2018
Roaster Bluestone Lane Coffee
Machine La Marzocco Linea PB, 2 groups
Grinder Mazzer Luigi Super Jolly

Espresso	$3.00
Cappuccino	$4.25
Latte	$4.25
Cold brew	$4.00

Bourgeois Pig

5931 Franklin Avenue, CA 90028 | **Hollywood**

Bourgeois Pig's kitschy, eccentric aesthetic betrays it as one of a dying breed in Los Angeles - an old school, 'the way it used to be' oasis for the coffee shop die hard. The shop is open 'til 2am, has plenty of electrical outlets, and will make you just about whatever you want - all rare qualities for a coffee shop these days. The mocha is especially delicious, as is the decaf, in case you're there late and averse to the effects of a fully caffeinated coffee.

(785) 843-1001
bourgeoispig.menutoeat.com

MON-SUN.   8:00am - 2:00am

First opened 1989
Roaster Blackwelder Coffee
Machine Slayer Espresso V3, 3 groups
Grinder Mazzer Luigi Robur E,
Mazzer Luigi Lux

Espresso	$4.50
Cappuccino	$5.50
Latte	$5.50
Cold brew	$5.00

Coffee Commissary Burbank

3121 West Olive Avenue, CA 91505 | **Burbank**

If you're seeking a place to gather with friends, this is a great one. Coava beans are on bar, creating a lovely, flavorful espresso experience that will leave you wanting more. The mocha is difficult to pass up, the chocolate pairing beautifully with the milk and espresso. The shop itself has an industrial feel with steel design elements, and wood furniture pieces soften the bolder aspects of the interior. Stop by for a nice environment, good service and great espresso.

(203) 448-9148
www.coffeecommissary.com

Sister locations Culver City / Glendale / Hollywood / Santa Monica / West Hollywood

MON–SUN. 7:00am – 8:00pm

First opened 2010
Roaster Multiple rotating roasters
Machine La Marzocco Strada, 3 groups
Grinder Mazzer Luigi Kony, Mazzer Luigi Robur

Espresso	$3.00
Cappuccino	$4.00
Latte	$4.25
Cold brew	$4.00

Coffee Commissary West Hollywood

801 North Fairfax Avenue, CA 90046 | **West Hollywood**

'In pursuit of the perfect cup' is Coffee Commissary's motto, and it lives up to it with flavorful espresso, friendly service and a captivating atmosphere in which to enjoy it all. A macchiato is an excellent menu choice, as it gives the Coava Roasters espresso the opportunity to stand on its own and really pop. Playful black and white doodles line the walls, and industrial design details help counter the whimsy with edgier elements. Coffee Commissary is a great place to grab your favorite coffee drink and deserves a visit if you're anywhere near Hollywood.

(323) 782-1465
coffeecommissary.com

Sister locations Burbank / Culver City / Glendale / Hollywood / Santa Monica

MON-FRI.	7:00am - 6:00pm
SAT-SUN.	7:00am - 5:00pm

First opened 2010
Roaster Multiple rotating roasters
Machine La Marzocco Strada, 3 groups
Grinder Mahlkönig Peak, Mahlkönig EK 43, Mazzer Luigi Robur, Mazzer Luigi Kony

Espresso	$3.00
Cappuccino	$4.00
Latte	$4.25
Cold brew	$4.00

Cuties Coffee

710 North Heliotrope Drive, CA 90029 | **Hollywood**

Obviously quirky from the moment you walk in, Cuties brings skill and unique passion to its coffee. It is also the only LGBTQ+ coffee shop in the city. One of the most notable aspects to this café is its 'community tab' system, a bowl filled with colorful tokens that represent one dollar that someone has given the shop to use for anyone who's short on cash and needs a helping hand. Cuties has a lot of heart, and it even uses Heart Roasters for its espresso! Full bodied and delicious, Heart Roasters makes a great base for the espresso offerings. Order a bottomless coffee to drink drip until you can't anymore.

(323) 539-3224
hicuties.com

MON-FRI.   8:00am – 3:00pm
SAT-SUN.   9:00am – 4:00pm

First opened 2017
Roaster Heart Coffee Roasters
Machine La Marzocco Linea EE, 2 groups
Grinder Mahlkönig EK 43, Mazzer Luigi Robur E

Espresso	$3.00
Cappuccino	$4.00
Latte	$5.00
Cold brew	$4.00

Javista Organic Coffee Bar

6707 Sunset Boulevard, CA 90028 | **Hollywood**

The mission of this café is in the name; 'Javista: A coffee fanatic. Someone who's always looking for a great coffee experience.' Javista does an amazing job of empowering the coffee obsessed by providing amazing products. This spot is extra popular, so you might have trouble finding a seat. The organic coffee offerings mean that a visit to Javista results in a truly elevated coffee experience - one free from harmful chemicals and pesticides. The lavender latte is an absolutely spectacular menu option; sweetness, floral notes and espresso mixing with milk to deliver a truly special caffeinated experience.

(323) 464-6707
javistacafe.com

MON-SUN. 7:00am - 7:00pm

First opened 2012
Roaster Urth Caffé
Machine Synesso MVP Hydra, 2 groups
Grinder Mazzer Luigi Robur

Espresso	$3.50
Cappuccino	$4.50
Latte	$4.75
Cold brew	$4.50

Joe & The Juice

8532 Melrose Avenue, CA 90069 | **West Hollywood**

LA locals find solace in this new venue, as it combines two of their favorite things - fresh pressed juices and great coffee. Danish in origin, this inspired café keeps you wanting more with its vast menu and makes it hard to leave the comfortable tables and seating. Joyful baristas and an enticing ambiance really makes this a great place to stop if you're in the area. Order an iced vanilla latte or green juice and leave satisfied. Whether you're into caffeine or healthy juices, or most likely both, Joe & The Juice is not your average cup of Joe.

joejuice.com

Sister locations Brentwood / Beverly Grove

MON-FRI.	6:00am - 9:00pm
SAT-SUN.	8:00am - 9:00pm

First opened 2017
Roaster Joe & The Juice
Machine La Marzocco Linea PB AV, 2 groups
Grinder Nuova Simonelli Mythos One

Espresso	$2.50
Cappuccino	$4.00
Latte	$4.40
Cold brew	$4.00

Philz Coffee

6430 Sunset Boulevard, CA 90028 | **Hollywood**

There are no lattes, nor espresso, just coffee. Rather than this detracting from the customer's experience, Philz does an incredible job of adding value to your order by having truly mastered the art of creating a classic cup of Joe. Each coffee is made to order, ensuring a fresh cup every time. The menu is full of fun additions, such as the iced mint mojito, which delivers a minty spin to your typical drip coffee. If you're feeling spunky, give the Tantalizing Turkish a try. If you're the kind who prefers to order 'just a coffee', Philz is your guy.

(323) 785-3001
www.philzcoffee.com

Sister locations Multiple locations

| MON-FRI. | 6:00am - 7:00pm |
| SAT-SUN. | 7:00am - 7:00pm |

First opened 2016
Roaster Philz Coffee
Grinder Ditting

Rubies+Diamonds

6115 West Sunset Boulevard #150, CA 90028 | **Hollywood**

Rubies+Diamonds takes glamorous to a new level with this large coffee space - crystal chandeliers and well-placed artwork sets the customer up for a luxurious coffee run. The only thing to make the experience even better is the coffee. Rubies+Diamonds uses its own beans, and each drink is well crafted; whether it's hot or iced, the skilful baristas will deliver you a truly satisfying brew. It offers many other signature coffee drinks, all of which offer a unique twist on classic favorites; grab a rose vanilla latte for something light, sweet and floral. Can't decide what to order? Choose the Nitro Flight and receive a perfect tasting board of their five delicious nitro options; cold brew, matcha latte, hibiscus, turmeric lemonade, and ginger ale. Stop at Rubies+Diamonds if you're looking for a shop with exceptional interior design and real pizzazz.

MON-SUN.   7:00am - 8:00pm

First opened 2016
Roaster Rubies+Diamonds
Machine La Marzocco Strada, 3 groups
Grinder Nuova Simonelli Mythos One

Espresso	$3.00
Cappuccino	$3.50
Latte	$4.50
Cold brew	$4.00

(323) 465-0400
www.rubiesanddiamonds.com

West Hollywood & Hollywood

Smith & Tait

866 Huntley Drive, CA 90069 | **West Hollywood**

The goal of the owners of Smith & Tait was to bring a piece of third wave coffee to the West Hollywood area. This little grab and go shop has a camping general store aesthetic and serves coffee that has a flavor so good it's hard to forget. Beans from Ritual means the espresso has great variety, as Ritual rotates by season. The turmeric latte used to be a secret menu item (Smith & Tait loves a good secret), but due to its popularity it's become a permanent member of the main menu. For an equally unique coffee option, the slightly sweet, and really smooth, frozen cold brew will not disappoint.

(424) 335-0359
www.smithandtait.com

MON-FRI. 7:00am - 5:00pm
SAT-SUN. 8:00am - 4:00pm

First opened 2016
Roaster Ritual Coffee Roasters
Machine La Marzocco FB80, 2 groups
Grinder Mahlkönig EK 43, Mazzer Luigi Robur, Mazzer Luigi Super Jolly

Espresso	$3.00
Cappuccino	$4.00
Latte	$4.50
Cold brew	$4.50

Verve Coffee Roasters Melrose Avenue

8925 Melrose Avenue, CA 90069 | **West Hollywood**

Between the stunning outdoor patio, the wide open indoor café space, the delicious coffee, and the great service, Verve has absolutely succeeded in bringing its popular Santa Cruz operation to flourish in LA. The nitro cold brew is smooth, flavorful and perfect for anyone who wants to elevate their traditional coffee order. The pour overs are also a delicious option, made with Verve's customary precision and care. If you're in the area, make sure to stop by, you'll be thankful you did.

(310) 385-9605
www.vervecoffee.com

Sister locations Spring Street / 3rd Street

MON-SUN. 7:00am - 8:00pm

First opened 2015
Roaster Verve Coffee Roasters
Machine Kees van der Westen Spirit, 4 groups
Grinder Nuova Simonelli Mythos x3

Espresso	$3.00
Cappuccino	$4.00
Latte	$4.75
Cold brew	$4.00

ROCKET
ESPRESSO MILANO

R NINE ONE

Culver City

Bar Nine

3515 Helms Avenue, CA 90232 | **Culver City**

Bar Nine is a sublime LA coffee spot, standing out with its sleek yet highly functional design. Exposed beams, concrete floor, a fully wooden bar and gleaming silver Modbar machines built into the counter give this beautifully large space an industrial/minimalist feel, allowing the incredibly fresh beans to take the main stage. A roastery/café par excellence, the coffee beans are roasted in front of you, with both single origin and blends being served on bar. Order a pour over made with the impressive Modbar system to elevate your coffee experience and grow your coffee knowledge here. Baristas are friendly and are sure to impress you with their skilful approach to coffee making. Come in early for a chance to secure a delicious pastry made by one of the owners, as they sell out quickly! Bar Nine really does raise the bar.

MON-SUN. 8:00am - 5:00pm

First opened 2014
Roaster Bar Nine
Machine Modbar, 2 groups
Grinder Mahlkönig EK 43

Espresso $4.50
Cappuccino $5.00
Latte $5.50
Cold brew $5.00

(310) 837-7815
barnine.us

Blue Bottle Coffee Hayden Tract

Platform, 8830 Washington Boulevard #103, CA 90232 | **Culver City**

Minimalist flair and purity in approach to coffee rules here, as always, at this Blue Bottle Culver City location within the trendy new Platform development. At first, this looks like a small take-out shop, and nothing wrong with that when the quality served is Blue Bottle. But step around behind bar and discover an impressive staged seating 'platform' overlooking an immense sunny outdoor terrace. What a great way to enjoy a New Orleans iced latte or a deliciously crafted single origin pour over. You'll probably want to take a bag of coffee to go or, even better, participate in the $20 brew classes every other Sunday. Then you'll be able to impress, just like the Blue Bottle barista pros.

(510) 653-3394
bluebottlecoffee.com

MON–SUN. 6:00am – 6:00pm

First opened 2016
Roaster Blue Bottle Coffee
Machine La Marzocco Strada, 2 groups
Grinder Mazzer Luigi Robur

Espresso	$3.50
Cappuccino	$4.50
Latte	$5.00
Cold brew	$4.00

Sister locations Multiple locations

The Boy & The Bear

12712 West Washington Boulevard, CA 90066 | **Culver City**

Walk into The Boy & The Bear and you'll immediately notice the ambiance; Edison light bulbs, a bit of natural light, and dark-colored decor create a moody atmosphere conducive to a feel-good coffee experience. Beyond decor, however, stands the self-roasted espresso - flavorful, bright, and consistently well-paired with milk. Grab a hemp milk latte for a dairy-free twist on a popular favorite or order a pour over for an expertly created cup. The baristas are friendly and knowledgeable about their beans, so strike up a conversation with them about their coffee menu. A visit to The Boy & The Bear is well worth your while.

theboyandthebear.com

Sister locations Redondo Beach

MON-SUN.   7:00am - 7:00pm

First opened 2018
Roaster The Boy & The Bear Specialty Coffee Roastery
Machine La Marzocco Strada, 3 groups
Grinder Mahlkönig EK 43

Espresso	$3.25
Cappuccino	$4.75
Latte	$4.75
Cold brew	$4.50

Cognoscenti Coffee Culver City

6114 Washington Boulevard, CA 90232 | **Culver City**

Cognoscenti is well regarded in the local coffee scene, and for good reason - multiple roasters are represented here, and the espresso quality is sublime. The baristas are friendly and especially knowledgeable when it comes to craft coffee. The interior of this Culver City location balances minimalist wooden furniture and bar design with an overall industrial feel, and also features plenty of interesting additions including brightly colored chairs. Order a V60 for a delicious pour over made on the Hario ceramic dripper and receive a perfectly prepared cup guaranteed to quench your coffee craving.

(310) 363-7325
cogcoffee.com

Sister locations South Park / Garment District

MON-SAT.	8:00am - 5:00pm
SUN.	9:00am - 3:00pm

First opened 2012
Roaster Ritual Coffee Roasters, Heart Coffee Roasters, Handsome Coffee and guests
Machine Kees van der Westen Spirit, 3 groups
Grinder Mahlkönig EK 43, Mazzer Luigi

Espresso	$3.00
Cappuccino	$3.75
Latte	$4.50
Cold brew	$4.00

Destroyer LA

3578 Hayden Avenue, CA 90232 | **Culver City**

Nestled within the Hayden Tract industrial estate in Culver City, Destroyer takes you on a taste journey. This is not surprising, given that this eatery/café is the brainchild of chef Jordan Khan of highly revered Vespertine - located literally across the street. You've no doubt come here for the sublime fine-casual food experience. The concise, seasonal menu projected onto the wall of this modern, minimalist space features items such as, roasted baby yams, beets with pumpkin seed butter and succulent chicken confit. The coffee offer is equally impressive. Try the delicious creamy cappuccino served in zen like earthenware, sparkling espresso by Roseline roasters prepared on the Mavam espresso machine, or raspberry and mint tonic. Destroyer is a bold and refined foodie establishment. This is an LA must visit and a superstar within the fast-evolving Culver City specialty coffee scene.

destroyer.la

MON-FRI.	8:00am - 5:00pm
SAT-SUN.	Closed

First opened 2016
Roaster Roseline Coffee
Machine Mavam, 2 groups
Grinder Mahlkönig, Nuova Simonelli Mythos One

Espresso	$3.00
Cappuccino	$4.00
Latte	$5.00

Venice

Blue Bottle Coffee Abbot Kinney

1103 Abbot Kinney Boulevard, CA 90291 | **Venice**

A cool, local spot for coffee, this compact Blue Bottle location stands out for its modern design and classic Blue Bottle aesthetic. Baristas are friendly, and the coffee is served with expert skill and knowhow. A wide variety of roasts showcase Blue Bottle's expertise and commitment to diverse flavors. The New Orleans Style Cold Brew is a stunning, truly alchemic drink that blends concentrated cold brew, organic cane sugar, roasted chicory, and your choice of milk to create a lightly sweet, refreshing drink experience. Perfectly central to the best this area has to offer, this Blue Bottle location is a great place to stop for a refreshment before a stroll along Abbot Kinney.

(510) 653-3394
bluebottlecoffee.com

Sister locations Multiple locations

MON-SUN. 5:30am - 7:00pm

First opened 2014
Roaster Blue Bottle Coffee
Machine Kees van der Westen Spirit, 2 groups
Grinder Mazzer Luigi Robur, Mahlkönig Peak

Espresso	$3.50
Cappuccino	$4.50
Latte	$4.50
Cold brew	$4.00

Bluestone Lane Surf Lifesaving Club

523 Rose Avenue, CA 90291 | **Venice**

Classy, refined, welcoming, and intimate - just a few words to describe Bluestone Lane's latest location in Venice, and its first outlet in Los Angeles with dinner service. This is an essential caffeine stop if you're nearby, offering exceptional espressos or flat whites that you're unlikely to forget. Ordering a breve macchiato is also a truly satisfying experience, with ultra-smooth and flavorful espresso notes emerging from the drink with every sip. Drawing inspiration from Bondi Beach cafés, the shop is designed to feel beachy and modern, and makes the transition from day to night with ease, featuring dimmed lighting and an extensive beer and wine menu. If you're looking for great coffee, delicious food, a beautiful atmosphere, and charming, friendly service, Bluestone Lane Surf Lifesaving Club is the café for you.

MON-THU.	7:30am - 10:30pm
FRI-SAT.	7:30am - 11:30pm
SUN.	8:00am - 10:30pm

Sister locations La Brea / Santa Monica / Studio City

First opened 2018
Roaster Bluestone Lane Coffee
Machine La Marzocco Linea PB, 2 groups
Grinder Mazzer Luigi Super Jolly, Mahlkönig EK 43

Espresso	$3.00
Cappuccino	$4.25
Latte	$4.25
Cold brew	$4.00

(718) 374-6858
bluestonelane.com

The Butcher's Daughter

1205 Abbot Kinney Boulevard, CA 90291 | **Venice**

One of the best spots in Venice to grab a bite to eat, The Butcher's Daughter brings its restaurant operation to a whole new level with its impressive espresso protocol. Working with Australian roaster Vittoria Coffee, they provide delicious coffee to their patrons, and every espresso drink is created at the 'Vittoria Coffee Espresso Bar'. The flat white is balanced and delectable and makes a great addition to your order if you're here to eat. There are often a few specialty lattes on the menu as well if you're looking for something a little more creative than your usual coffee order. The space itself is large and welcoming, designed to perfection by the owner herself. Stop here if you're looking for a high-quality, well-rounded coffee and food experience.

(310) 981-3004
www.thebutchersdaughter.com

MON-SUN.   8:00am - 10:00pm

First opened 2016
Roaster Vittoria Coffee
Machine Faema E61, 2 groups
Grinder Bunn

Espresso	$3.50
Cappuccino	$5.00
Latte	$5.00
Cold brew	$4.50

Deus Café

1001 Venice Boulevard, CA 90291 | **Venice**

This open-air coffee venue does a great job of blending its motorbike and surfing shop with its coffee hang-out by creating a casual and friendly environment with rugged and industrial-style design. The three-group Faema brings out the best in the Vittoria espresso blend, and the baristas are skilled at coaxing great flavor out of the beans. Order a coffee with CBD oil to help curb your stress or opt for the affogato for a midday treat. Parking and seating is plentiful, so this is a great place to stick around and get work done before you go for that ride.

(888) 515-3387
deuscustoms.com/cafes/venice/

MON-SUN.   7:00am - 7:00pm

First opened 2011
Roaster Vittoria Coffee
Machine Faema Teorema, 3 groups
Grinder Mazzer Luigi Super Jolly

Espresso	$3.00
Cappuccino	$3.75
Latte	$4.00
Cold brew	$4.00

Flowerboy Project

824 Lincoln Boulevard, CA 90291 | **Venice**

Step inside Flowerboy Project and be transported to a secret garden hidden just a few streets over from Abbot Kinney Boulevard. This is the result of Sean Knibb's work as a designer, his studio just next door, and the inspiration he gathered from growing up in his Grandmother's flower shop. With a thoughtful selection of flower varietals available for purchase, crystals lining the counters, and children's alphabet magnets spelling out the menu, Flowerboy stands out with its creative attention to detail. The 'Rose Girl' latte really shines as a clever and delicious drink, its light floral notes mixing beautifully with the delicious espresso.

(310) 452-3900
www.flowerboyproject.com

Sister locations DTLA

MON-SUN.   7:00am – 5:00pm

First opened 2015
Roaster Counter Culture Coffee
Machine La Marzocco Linea, 2 groups
Grinder Bunn

Espresso	$3.50
Cappuccino	$4.00
Latte	$4.50
Cold brew	$4.00

Gjusta

320 Sunset Avenue, CA 90291 | **Venice**

Step inside this all-day café and encounter a sprawling warehouse space that transports you to an earlier, simpler time. This is a bakery and deli in every sense of the word, with almost every food option you could imagine. At the end of the long counter is a large coffee bar, the La Marzocco espresso machine gleaming with the promise of a delicious cup. The cold brew is zingy and full bodied and is paired beautifully with one of the house-made pastries to start your day off right. Seating outside is a popular option for enjoying coffee, but the large marble standing bar by the coffee machine is also a lovely place to enjoy your brew.

(310) 314-0320
gjusta.com

Sister locations Gjelina / GTA

MON-SUN. 7:00am - 10:00pm

First opened 2014
Roaster Common Room Roasters
Machine La Marzocco Linea PB, 3 groups
Grinder Mahlkönig EK 43, Mazzer Luigi

Espresso	$3.50
Cappuccino	$5.00
Latte	$5.00
Cold brew	$5.00

Great White

1604 Pacific Avenue, CA 90291 | **Venice**

Sandy feet and swimsuits are more than welcome in this beachy café located in the heart of Venice Beach. Step in to Aussie-inspired Great White for a post swim pick-me-up and refuel with some of the best coffee in the area. The atmosphere is comfortable yet chic, and the seating is predominantly light wooden stools, both high at the bar and lower at marble topped tables. Everything about this stunning venue is welcoming and relaxed; it's an incredible space for meeting up with a friend or hanging out to refuel after your beach day. Sit up at the bar and watch the skilled baristas work their magic, it is truly a pleasure to observe. Come by around mealtime and be greeted by a fresh and delicious fare of healthy and hearty breakfast, brunch and lunch dishes. Order a flat white and relax in Great White's open-air seating area full of fresh ocean breeze.

MON-SUN. 7:00am – 5:00pm

First opened 2017
Roaster Vittoria Coffee
Machine Faema E71, 2 groups
Grinder Mazzer Luigi

Espresso	$3.00
Cappuccino	$4.50
Latte	$4.50
Cold brew	$6.00

(424) 744-8403
greatwhitevenice.com

Intelligentsia Coffee Venice Coffeebar

1331 Abbot Kinney Boulevard, CA 90291 | **Venice**

Sandwiched between two shops on the popular Abbot Kinney Boulevard is the legendary Venice location of Intelligentsia, the Chicago-based coffee roaster that brings an authentic, rough-around-the-edges vibe to the Los Angeles coffee scene. You'll know you've found it when you see the blinking neon sign depicting a steaming coffee cup. Featuring plenty of counter space and a sea of business professionals behind laptops, this shop is a popular workspace. Open ceilings with exposed beams above a plexi-glass overhang gives this shop a wicked industrial feel. Intelligentsia serves coffee from its own roastery, and ordering any espresso-based drink will ensure you're drinking experience is exemplary, or choose a pour over for a delicately fragrant brew. If you're looking for something a little sweeter than a coffee, the semi-sweet, semi-spicy chai is a great alternative. Make sure to pick up one of the fresh baked goods too, you'll be thankful you did.

MON-THU.	6:00am - 8:00pm
FRI.	6:00am - 10:00pm
SAT.	7:00am - 10:00pm
SUN.	7:00am - 8:00pm

Sister locations Silver Lake / Pasadena / Hollywood (coming soon)

First opened 2009
Roaster Intelligentsia
Machine Synesso, 2 groups x2
Grinder Mazzer Luigi x4

Espresso	$3.50
Cappuccino	$4.25
Latte	$4.50
Cold brew	$4.50

(310) 399-1233
www.intelligentsiacoffee.com

Menotti's Coffee Stop

56 Windward Avenue, CA 90291 | **Venice**

MON-SUN.   7:00am - 6:00pm

While Menotti's looks unassuming from the outside, don't be fooled - walk through the door to reveal its impressive atmosphere that features a relaxed, yet clean design, as well as delicious, well-crafted espresso. The friendly baristas do an incredible job of making you a drink that you'll truly relish. Order a Spanish latte if you're looking for something on the sweet side, or the single-origin Costa Rican espresso for a smooth, full-bodied traditional espresso experience. Steps away from Venice Beach, stop at Menotti's for a truly beautiful brew.

(424) 205-7014
www.menottiscoffeeveniceca.com

First opened 2013
Roaster Cat & Cloud Coffee,
Verve Coffee Roasters
Machine La Marzocco Linea Mini, 2 groups
Grinder Mahlkönig EK 43,
Mazzer Luigi Major x2

Espresso	$3.50
Cappuccino	$4.00
Latte	$4.50 / $5.00
Cold brew	$4.50

TOMS Roasting Co.

1344 Abbot Kinney Boulevard, CA 90291 | **Venice**

For every cup sold, someone in the developing world is getting clean water. On top of having particularly delicious espresso and really friendly baristas, TOMS flagship store in Venice is a great place to stop for a brew. There's both indoor seating, as well as covered outdoor space. Of course, TOMS shoes feature for sale here, as the coffee shop doubles as a shoe store (also supporting charity). With lots of outlets, this is a great place to get some work done. Grab a bag of coffee on your way out - each bag sold results in 140 liters of clean water for a family in coffee producing regions.

(310) 314-9700
www.toms.com

Sister locations Glendale

| MON-FRI. | 6:00am - 8:00pm |
| SAT-SUN. | 7:00am - 8:00pm |

First opened 2012
Roaster TOMS Roasting Co.
Machine La Marzocco Linea, 3 groups
Grinder Mahlkönig K30 Twin

Espresso	$2.75
Cappuccino	$4.00
Latte	$4.25
Cold brew	$4.00

Santa Monica & Brentwood

Balconi Coffee Company

11301 West Olympic Boulevard #124, CA 90064 | **Sawtelle**

Balconi is a beautiful blend of kitschy and classy. Between the impressive siphon coffee brewers, vintage espresso machine, coffee beans from Verve, and art lining the walls, this shop is keeping it unique. Order a single origin Kenya siphon coffee for a bright and robust cup. This is a popular spot, but with so much seating you shouldn't have trouble finding a place to get comfy in. The barista's attention to detail is outstanding and ensures a high-quality coffee experience every time you visit.

(310) 906-0267
www.balconicoffeecompany.com

MON-FRI.	7:00am - 10:00pm
SAT-SUN.	10:00am - 10:00pm

First opened 2011
Roaster Balconi Coffee Company, Tectonic Coffee Co., Verve Coffee Roasters
Machine La Marzocco Linea, 2 groups
Grinder Mahlkönig K30 Twin, Mahlkönig Peak

Espresso	$3.00
Cappuccino	$4.00
Latte	$4.50
Cold brew	$4.00

Blue Bottle Coffee Brentwood

13050 San Vicente Boulevard, CA 90049 | **Brentwood**

Bringing a little taste of San Francisco to Los Angeles, Blue Bottle's sweet and compact Brentwood location is a great addition to the neighborhood. Assorted pastries fill the clear case, and drinks made on the La Marzocco espresso machine are crafted to perfection. Cappuccinos are delicious, Blue Bottle's smoky roast is highlighted by a perfect espresso-to-milk ratio. The service is exceptional, and the beans are outstanding no matter the method; order a pour over and sit out in the beautiful sunshine. Perfectionists in all areas, Blue Bottle leave nothing to chance.

(510) 653-3394
bluebottlecoffee.com

Sister locations Multiple locations

MON-SUN.   6:00am - 6:00pm

First opened 2017
Roaster Blue Bottle Coffee
Machine La Marzocco Linea PB, 3 groups
Grinder Mazzer Luigi Robur

Espresso	$3.50
Cappuccino	$4.50
Latte	$5.00
Cold brew	$4.00

Bluestone Lane Santa Monica

631 Wilshire Boulevard, CA 90401 | **Santa Monica**

This location of the New York-based Bluestone Lane leaves a great first impression. Saying that it was thoughtfully designed doesn't even begin to describe the immaculate interior, which features a stunning color palette and pleasant decorative accents. The wall of potted plants on the patio continues this design theme and creates a tranquil atmosphere in which to drink your favorite coffee.
This Aussie-inspired shop knows how to do a flat white justice - order one and receive a smooth, perfectly roasted, and expertly crafted cup.

(718) 374-6858
bluestonelane.com

Sister locations La Brea / Venice / Studio City

MON-SUN.   7:00am - 6:00pm

First opened 2018
Roaster Bluestone Lane Coffee
Machine La Marzocco Linea PB, 2 groups
Grinder Mazzer Luigi Super Jolly

Espresso	$3.00
Cappuccino	$4.25
Latte	$4.25
Cold brew	$4.00

Bulletproof Coffee

3310 Main Street, CA 90405 | **Ocean Park**

Just a hop and a skip away from the Santa Monica beach is Bulletproof, the coffee shop branch of this infamous health brand of the same name. The shop specializes in coffee with added fats that can supposedly support weight loss. The coffee, MCT oil and butter concoction creates a nutty, almost caramel flavor. Lots of delicious and healthy food options showcase Bulletproof's interest in providing a well-rounded experience for its patrons. Its ingenuity and niche coffee offerings make visiting this shop a truly unique experience for everyone who stops by.

(310) 399-1764
bluebottlecoffee.com

Sister locations DTLA

MON-SUN.   6:00am - 8:00pm

First opened 2016
Roaster Bulletproof Coffee
Machine La Marzocco Linea
Grinder Mahlkönig Guatemala

Espresso	$3.00
Cappuccino	$5.75
Latte	$5.50 / $6.00
Cold brew	$5.00

Caffe Luxxe

225 26th Street, CA 90402 | **Brentwood**

The quality this shop brings to its beverages is apparent from the first sip - you can truly taste and see all the attention put into each cup. The compact café space itself is stunning; the sleek and minimal interior really serves to make your morning coffee even more spectacular. The outdoor seating is plentiful, and the shop even features a gift bar area in case you're in need of any small tokens of appreciation for someone special in your life. The baristas put a lot of care to ensure that each shot of espresso is right, and this gives Caffe Luxxe a definite appeal to any true coffee aficionado. This Brentwood location of Luxxe is beautiful, and definitely worth a visit.

(310) 394-2222
www.caffeluxxe.com

MON-SUN. 7:00am - 6:00pm

First opened 2010
Roaster Caffe Luxxe
Machine Synesso Cyncra, 2 groups
Grinder Mazzer Luigi Robur E

Espresso $3.25
Cappuccino $4.50
Latte $4.75

Sister locations Multiple locations

Espresso Cielo

1431 2nd Street, CA 90401 | **Santa Monica**

The design of this Santa Monica shop has a definite French café feel, and as the first Los Angeles shop to serve coffee from the Canadian roasters, 49th Parallel, Espresso Cielo's core elements are internationally influenced. Cool design tones and a wide-open space with big windows makes this location of Espresso Cielo especially welcoming. The espresso blend on bar is a full-bodied dark roast that expresses notes of deep chocolate. Order a cappuccino for an excellently crafted espresso-based beverage before a stroll along the water.

(310) 260-1268
espressocielo.com

Sister locations Santa Monica
(Main Street)

MON–SUN.   7:00am – 6:00pm

First opened 2017
Roaster 49th Parallel Coffee Roasters
Machine Synesso MVP Hydra, 3 groups
Grinder Mahlkönig EK 43

Espresso	$3.25
Cappuccino	$4.50
Latte	$4.50 / $5.00 / $5.50
Cold brew	$5.00

Espresso Profeta

1129 Glendon Avenue, CA 90024 | **Westwood**

Classy and cute, head to Espresso Profeta for a well-rounded coffee experience in an environment surrounded by exposed brick and modern art. The espresso is especially of note, prepared excellently on the two-group Synesso machine. If you're looking for something on the bolder side, the Italiano is the drink for you. This coffee is some of the best in Westwood, and deserves a stop whenever you're in the area.

(310) 208-3375
www.espressoprofetalosangeles.com

MON–SUN. 7:00am – 7:00pm

First opened 2006
Roaster Espresso Vivace
Machine Synesso Cyncra, 2 groups
Grinder Mazzer Luigi Robur E

Espresso	$3.00
Cappuccino	$4.00
Latte	$4.50
Cold brew	$4.75

Good People Coffee Co

11609 Santa Monica Boulevard, CA 90025 | **Sawtelle**

Exposed brick walls and quirky black and white designs make this shop immediately interesting before you even open the door. The drip coffee is of note, offering a bright and tangy cup and the Sanremo Opera machine brings out the very best in the espresso. The house-made hazelnut milk (listed as 'the good nut milk' on the menu) is a great dairy alternative and tastes just as wonderful in an iced latte. Good People Coffee Co is committed to making you a cup of coffee you'll adore, and the baristas love if you ask questions about their interesting food and coffee menu. In sharing their passion with you, you are sure to leave having had an excellent, immersive experience. Good People, great coffee.

www.goodpeoplecoffeeco.com

MON-SAT.	7:00am - 4:00pm
SUN.	8:00am - 3:00pm

First opened 2018
Roaster Lift Coffee Roasters, Alana's Coffee Roasters, Onyx Coffee Lab
Machine Sanremo Opera 2.0, 2 groups
Grinder Fiorenzato F83

Espresso	$3.50
Cappuccino	$4.50
Latte	$5.50
Cold brew	$5.00

goodboybob coffee

2058 Broadway, CA 90404 | **Mid-City**

goodboybob is a hidden Santa Monica gem. Unlike many modern coffee shops designed to keep traffic moving by making seating difficult to sit on for long periods, goodboybob is full of couches and comfy seats that serve to make coffee drinkers feel cozy and comfortable. It's so well-designed, in fact, that it makes an excellent co-working space or sophisticated lounge area. The design aesthetic is like a modern living room; exposed wood, warm tones, and plenty of seating defines the space and makes patrons feel at home. Fresh flowers are all around the shop, and the bar is open and welcoming. Order anything with espresso for a beautiful brew and experience a full-bodied flavor that pairs great with milk.

MON-FRI.	7:00am - 4:00pm
SAT-SUN.	8:00am - 12:00pm

First opened 2017
Roaster goodboybob coffee
Machine La Marzocco Strada AV, 3 groups
Grinder Nuova Simonelli Mythos One Clima Pro x2

Espresso	$3.50
Cappuccino	$4.00
Latte	$4.50
Cold brew	$5.00

(818) 452-5495
www.goodboybob.com

Groundwork Coffee Co. Santa Monica

2908 Main Street, CA 90405 | **Ocean Park**

This nearly 30-year-old café is a true mainstay of the Rose Avenue neighborhood. Offering a cozy environment for working or catching up with friends, this shop is often packed full of people. Groundwork was one of the first organic roasters in California and has grown to feature its products in local grocery stores. Try the cold brew for a cool and refreshing coffee hit or grab an espresso-based drink for something dependably delicious and well made. Baristas here are down to earth and are sure to make you something you'll love with every visit.

(310) 452-8925
www.groundworkcoffee.com

Sister locations Multiple locations

MON–SUN. 6:00am – 6:00pm

First opened 2003
Roaster Groundwork Coffee Co.
Machine La Marzocco GB5 EE, 2 groups
Grinder Mahlkönig K30 Twin

Espresso	$3.25
Cappuccino	$4.25
Latte	$4.75
Cold brew	$4.50

Kiff Kafe

12229 West Pico Boulevard, CA 90064 | **Sawtelle**

MON-SUN. 7:30am – 5:00pm

Kiff Kafe has a really clean feel, with an outdoor patio area full of plants and seating. The shop has an elevated ambiance, like someone took a favorite neighborhood coffee shop and brought it to a whole new level. Kiff keeps it local by using beans roasted by the Los Angeles company Pasquini and brings out all the right flavors with its espresso protocol. Pair your well-executed coffee with a deliciously fresh plate if you're there around meal time. Come here when the weather is mild and enjoy the bright open space with plenty of room to hang out.

(424) 293-2885
www.kiffkafe.com

First opened 2018
Roaster Pasquini Coffee Co
Machine Faema Teorema, 2 groups
Grinder Casadio Enea

Espresso	$3.25
Cappuccino	$4.00
Latte	$4.50
Cold brew	$4.00

Pasadena & Surrounding

CITY HALL

Again Cafe

132 West Green Street, CA 91105 | **Pasadena**

In the heart of Old Town Pasadena sits Again Café, a modern addition to the classic neighborhood that surrounds it. Again has tons of creative menu options, expanding beyond its coffee menu into delicious iced teas, colorful lemonades and chai. In the evening this café becomes a ramen bar and everything you order is sure to be tasty. The shop is designed simply but holds to a sleek aesthetic, providing a great environment in which to enjoy your latte. Options are truly endless here and the espresso is on point, making this a must-try outer Los Angeles coffee destination.

(626) 999-4794
chibiscus.com

MON-SUN.   8:00am - 3:00pm

First opened 2017
Roaster Tectonic Coffee Co.
Machine La Marzocco Linea PB AV, 2 groups
Grinder Nuova Simonelli Mythos One Clima Pro

Espresso	$3.00
Cappuccino	$4.00
Latte	$4.50
Cold brew	$4.00

Black Elephant Coffee

3195 Glendale Boulevard, CA 90039 | **Atwater Village**

Black Elephant was designed to facilitate a strong sense of community and the enjoyment of a great cup of coffee. Positioned in the middle of the café is a long communal table; a great place to get work done, or to visit with one of the kindred coffee drinkers sitting with you. The baristas are more than friendly, you can tell how much they enjoy working here. Anything you order is lovingly prepared, but the single origin drip from Stumptown is especially of note and showcases phenomenally robust and smooth flavor notes. Job done!

(323) 486-7848
www.blackelephantcoffee.com

MON-FRI.	7:00am - 6:00pm
SAT-SUN.	8:00am - 6:00pm

First opened 2018
Roaster Stumptown Coffee Roasters
Machine La Marzocco Linea, 2 groups
Grinder Mazzer Luigi Kony, Bunn

Espresso	$3.00
Cappuccino	$4.00
Latte	$4.50
Cold brew	$4.25

Civil Coffee

5629 North Figueroa Street, CA 90042 | **Highland Park**

Photo: David Maziarz

Civil Coffee is one of only a couple of coffee shops in the small Highland Park neighborhood, but even so, it has set a high bar for quality for the surrounding shops. The espresso from Heart Roasters is brewed to perfection here, and the environment in which you get to enjoy your coffee is dynamic and truly beautiful. All the baristas are extremely helpful and are sure to make you a coffee that fits your taste preference. The Arroyo, a lavender latte that is lightly sweet and delicately floral, goes great with a pastry, but if you're looking for something a little richer, the One and One, equal parts milk and espresso, is a stunning demonstration of Heart's flavorful roast. This is a great place to bring a book or a journal and relax while sipping your beautiful brew.

MON-SUN.   6:30am – 5:30pm

First opened 2015
Roaster Coava Coffee Roasters, Heart Coffee Roasters and guests
Machine La Marzocco GB5, 2 groups
Grinder Mazzer Luigi Robur E

Espresso	$3.50
Cappuccino	$4.00
Latte	$4.50
Cold brew	$4.00

civilcoffee.com

Collage Coffee

5106 York Boulevard, CA 90042 | **Eagle Rock**

Collage Coffee brings creativity and color to the growing Highland Park coffee scene with aesthetically pleasing beverage options and a cool shop design. The outside of the shop is a mosaic of brightly colored tile that immediately alerts patrons to the playful nature of the venue, and the theme continues inside, creating a really lovely atmosphere. If you're not sure what to order, give the iced latte a try - the espresso from Ruby Roasters pairs very well with any of the milk options. Whether you're looking to sit in and relax or grab and go, Collage Coffee has you covered.

(323) 682-8206
www.collagecoffee.com

MON-SUN.   7:00am - 3:00pm

First opened 2017
Roaster Ruby Coffee Roasters
Machine La Marzocco Linea PB, 2 groups
Grinder Mahlkönig EK 43, Mazzer Luigi

Espresso	$3.25
Cappuccino	$4.00
Latte	$4.25
Cold brew	$4.00

Copa Vida

70 South Raymond Avenue, CA 91105 | **Pasadena**

Bright and open, Copa Vida in Old Pasadena is a popular destination for friends and freelancers alike. This location is often bustling with activity, and we can see why. It makes an excellent cortado; the beans Copa Vida roasts are packed full of flavor and pair well with milk. The food is also excellent; coming here for lunch and finishing off with a coffee is a great way to experience all the goodness that Copa Vida has to offer.

(626) 213-3952
copa-vida.com

Sister locations Glendora

MON-SUN. 7:00am - 10:00pm

First opened 2013
Roaster Copa Vida Coffee
Machine Kees van der Westen Spirit, 3 groups, Alpha Dominche Steampunk
Grinder Mahlkönig EK 43, Mazzer Luigi Kony E x2

Espresso	$3.00
Cappuccino	$4.00
Latte	$4.50
Cold brew	$4.00

Found Coffee

1335 Colorado Boulevard, CA 90041 | **Eagle Rock**

Bright and modern, Found Coffee brings some extra shine and deliciousness to the Eagle Rock neighborhood. The drink options are wonderfully unique and the baristas are friendly and helpful. Plenty of seating means you won't have any problem settling in and getting cozy. Found is a multi-roaster specialty coffee shop, which enables it to keep its coffee offerings fresh and diverse. Order the bourbon vanilla latte for a truly artisanal coffee cocktail or opt for a cold brew for a refreshing palate-pleaser.

(323) 206-5154
www.foundcoffeela.com

Sister locations FrankieLucy (Silver Lake)

MON-SUN.   7:00am - 6:00pm

First opened 2015
Roaster Demitasse, Stereoscope Coffee Co, Peri Coffee and guests
Machine La Marzocco GB5 EE, 2 groups
Grinder Mahlkönig EK 43, Nuova Simonelli Mythos, Ditting

Espresso	$3.00
Cappuccino	$3.75
Latte	$4.50
Cold brew	$4.00

Highlight Coffee

701 East Broadway, CA 91205 | **Citrus Grove**

Your morning is easily spent at this sweet Citrus Grove hideaway, with sun filtering through the large windows, a delicious cup of coffee, and friendly service to set the tone for the rest of your day. The coffee bar extends to both sides of the shop which opens up the space and creates an exceedingly pleasant atmosphere. The butterscotch latte is sweet and delicious and makes a great order if you're looking for something unique. However, for a more traditional brew, the single origin pour over is a great option. Highlight is a multi-roaster café, so you'll have no trouble finding a special coffee option to adore.

(818) 484-8414
www.highlightcoffee.com

MON-FRI.	6:30am - 8:00pm
SAT-SUN.	8:00am - 8:00pm

First opened 2016
Roaster Sweet Bloom Coffee Roasters, Phil & Sebastian, Demitasse Coffee Roasters
Machine La Marzocco Linea PB ABR, 2 groups
Grinder Mahlkönig Kenia, Anfim SCODY II, Nuova Simonelli Mythos One x2

Espresso	$3.25
Cappuccino	$4.00
Latte	$4.25
Cold brew	$4.00

Kindness & Mischief Coffee

5537 North Figueroa Street, CA 90042 | **Highland Park**

Featuring simple and chic interior design, a thoughtfully curated menu of coffee offerings, and some of the friendliest service you can find, Kindness & Mischief is taking Highland Park by storm.
Its espresso is excellent, each cup is smooth and flavorful. If you're feeling particularly giving, order the 'kindness cup', a menu option that enables you to pay it forward and pay for someone else's drink. Order 'The Mischief' for a latte brought to a new level with chocolate and spice. Lots of outlets line the walls, making this a great place to buckle down and get some work done too. Stop by and watch Kindness & Mischief become one of your Los Angeles favorites.

www.kandmcoffee.com

MON-SUN. 7:00am - 5:00pm

First opened 2016
Roaster Multiple roasters
Machine La Marzocco GB5, 2 groups
Grinder Mahlkönig K30 Air, Mahlkönig EK 43

Espresso	$3.00
Cappuccino	$4.00
Latte	$4.50
Cold brew	$4.00

Pasadena & Surrounding

TOP **40**

Little Ripper Coffee

4155 Verdugo Road, CA 90065 | **Eagle Rock**

Little Ripper is bright and beautiful with its suave interior, creating a lovely space in which to enjoy your coffee. A wave design adorns the back wall of the bar, white tile lines the counters, and a few well-placed plants makes this a lovely space to sit and relax. The cold brew is superb, with a smooth, well-rounded flavor profile. Order the 'Little Ripper' for a unique experience that features iced espresso with a house made lavender date-sweetened almond milk. Aussie-inspired shops are making serious waves in the Los Angeles coffee scene, and Little Ripper is no exception.

(323) 739-0328
littlerippercoffee.com

MON-FRI. 7:00am - 3:00pm
SAT-SUN. 8:00am - 4:00pm

First opened 2017
Roaster La Colombe Coffee Roasters
Machine La Marzocco Linea EE, 2 groups
Grinder Mahlkönig

Espresso	$3.00
Cappuccino	$4.00
Latte	$4.50
Cold brew	$4.00

Rosebud Coffee

2302 East Colorado Boulevard, CA 91107 | **Lamanda Park**

Rosebud began as a coffee cart with the special mission to empower homeless and transitional-aged youth. As it has grown, so has its ability to reach out to the local community and provide meaningful employment options to the disenfranchised. Rosebud uses Wild Goose coffee, and sources salads and sandwiches (a real must try) from Hope, continuing its commitment to the community by partnering with suppliers who are just as dedicated to making a difference and supporting those less fortunate.
The employees here are truly skilled baristas, delivering delicious espresso-based beverages adorned with stunning latte art. The full flavor profile of the Wild Goose beans can be seen best in a stunning pour over, so make sure to sample this if you have time to stop and smell the coffee. The design of the shop is captivatingly minimal and aesthetic, with beautiful art adorning the walls and plenty of seating throughout. If you want to participate in 'coffee with a cause', don't miss this gem in Pasadena.

MON–FRI.	7:00am – 5:00pm
SAT.	7:00am – 11:00am
SUN.	Closed

Pasadena & Surrounding

First opened 2017
Roaster Wild Goose Coffee Roasters
Machine La Marzocco Linea PB, 2 groups
Grinder Mahlkönig EK 43, Mahlkönig K30
Vario Air, Mazzer Luigi, Baratza Sette 270

Espresso	$2.75
Cappuccino	$3.50
Latte	$4.25
Cold brew	$5.00

(626) 817-3461
www.rosebudcoffee.com

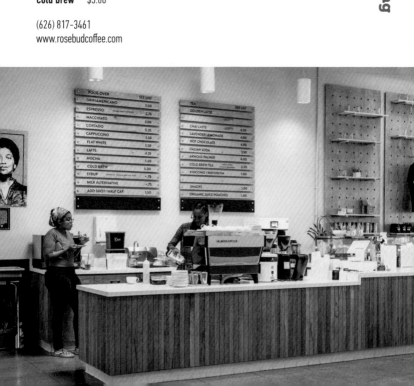

The Los Angeles Coffee Festival

PROUDLY

NOVEMBER 2019

Los Angeles' Flagship Coffee Event

 @LACoffeeFest 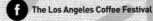 The Los Angeles Coffee Festival @losangelescoffeefestival

SUPPORTING

PROJECT WATER FALL

BRINGING CLEAN WATER
TO COFFEE GROWING COMMUNITIES

projectwaterfall.org

 @projectwaterf   Project Waterfall   @project_waterfall

Behind every cup of coffee is a unique story. On its journey from coffee tree to cup, coffee passes through the hands of a number of skilled individuals. Over the following pages, expert contributors share their specialist knowledge. As you will see, the coffee we enjoy is the result of a rich and complex process, and there is always something new to learn.

Coffee
Knowledge

Photo: Horst A. Friedrichs

Coffee at Origin

by **Mike Riley**, Falcon Speciality Green Coffee Importers

If you go into New York's vibrant coffee community today and ask any good barista what makes a perfect cup of coffee, they will always tell you that it starts with the bean. Beyond the roasting technique, the perfect grind, and exact temperatures and precision pressure of a modern espresso machine, we must look to the dedicated coffee farmer who toils away in the tropical lands of Africa, Asia and Latin America. They are the first heroes of our trade.

Approximately 25 million people in over 50 countries are involved in producing coffee. The bean, or seed to be exact, is extracted from cherries that most commonly ripen red but sometimes orange or yellow. The cherries are usually hand-picked then processed by various means. Sometimes they are dried in the fruit under tropical sunshine until they resemble raisins - a process known as 'natural'. The 'honey process' involves pulping the fresh cherries to extract the beans which are then sundried, still coated in their sticky mucilage. Alternatively, in the 'washed process', the freshly pulped beans are left to stand in tanks of water for several hours where enzyme activity breaks down the mucilage, before they are sundried on concrete patios or raised beds. Each method has a profound impact on the ultimate flavor of the coffee.

The term 'speciality coffee' is used to differentiate the world's best from the rest. This means it has to be Arabica, the species of coffee that is often bestowed with incredible flavors - unlike its hardy cousin Robusta which is usually reserved for commercial products and many instant blends. But being Arabica alone is by no means enough for a coffee to achieve the speciality tag, since the best beans are usually those grown at higher altitude on rich and fertile soils. As well as country and region of origin, the variety is important too; Bourbon, Typica, Caturra, Catuai, Pacamara and Geisha to name but a few. Just as Shiraz and Chardonnay grapes have their own complex flavors, the same is true of coffee's varieties. Some of the world's most amazing coffees are the result of the farmer's innovative approach to experimentation with growing and production techniques, meaning that today's speciality roaster is able to source coffees of incredible complexity and variation.

A good coffee establishment will showcase coffees when they are at their best - freshly harvested and seasonal, just like good fruit and vegetables. Seasonal espresso blends change throughout the year to reflect this.

As speciality coffee importers we source stand-out coffees by regularly travelling to origin countries. Direct trade with farmers is always our aim. Above all, we pay sustainable prices and encourage them to treat their land, and those who work it, with respect. Such an approach is increasingly demanded by New York's speciality coffee community in order to safeguard the industry's future.

161

Small Batch Roasting

by **Jonathan Withers**, Green Coffee Buyer, Toby's Estate Coffee Roasters

....

Coffee roasted in small batches is a pillar of the specialty coffee industry. It's an essential part of how we elevate our product above the classic American perception of coffee as a simple common commodity. At Toby's Estate, we and our customers celebrate a small batch methodology. It is an artisanal, hand-crafted approach that facilitates and advances deep connections between tradesperson and material, removed from the industrial construct of mass production prioritized above quality; fostering instead a relationship with the client centered on a product made-to-order, carefully and skillfully.

Successfully delivering quality with this approach relies on the implementation of systems which are focused towards consistently achieving a high standard - batch to batch and day to day. From the perspective of the customer, quality is only as high as our ability to fulfill every time. Among the artisanal aspects of small batch roasting, experienced craftspeople have the tools at hand to achieve these high degrees of quality; it's only a matter of applying them towards the goal of consistency.

The operation of small batch equipment allows for the manipulation of multiple controls towards the progress and outcome of a roast: heat via gas burners, airflow via fan speed, damper position, drum speed, and chosen batch size. These variables all independently influence the roast and are essential

avenues for exploration in obtaining the sweet-spot. That is the reference profile of how to best roast that coffee in production. Too many variables moving at once however, will diminish the roaster's control over the batch. Once this ideal roasting of a coffee is established, reducing the complexity of variables is key. In most production machines, this is commonly achieved by setting all variables other than gas pressure. Then the batch is controlled solely by manipulating the heat applied to the roaster.

Having limited the variables to simplify and improve repeatability, we need points of feedback with which to monitor and react to controls and results during the roast. Temperature readings at multiple points in the roasting system are essential. These are done with a probe that measures the air exiting the drum and a probe placed awash in the beans to measure the temperature of coffee mass. Gauges on the gas supply and roaster exhaust air allow for hard measurements of the values of heat being applied (burners) and removed (airflow). Associating a reference profile to a static batch size allows these values to serve as a meaningful reference. Therefore, we can replicate the precise conditions and adjustments in future production batches. For recording, collating, and parsing all this data, many options exist to digitally log roasting data and display the information as a referable curve. By drawing the current curve over that of the reference, batches can be skillfully manipulated to be precisely replicated.

After the batch is dropped and cooled, other points to control consistency exist to ensure perfect uniformity. Measuring the weight of the roasted coffee against that of the initial green shows the moisture mass lost during roasting. This number will change as the green coffee ages throughout its lifespan, but from day to day it provides a simple metric as to how similarly the coffee was roasted. More precisely, color analyzers exist which optically meter roasted, ground coffee to give a numeric value indicating the degree to which the coffee has roasted. Cupping your roasted product is of course the most direct connection with the success of the final consistency.

Multiple batches appearing together on the same table are incredibly meaningful as they can be directly compared against one another. Carefully recording and collating this sensory data allows a full picture of success as well as areas for focused improvements.

Successfully delivering quality from small batch roasting relies on the skills, talent, and experience of the operator. Yet to ensure that this artistry is maintained and guaranteed with every batch over long days and weeks, a rigorous system of variable control, monitoring metrics and tight quality control is paramount. When they catch problems, you're glad the mistakes weren't able to slip through the cracks.

Water - The Enigma

by **Maxwell Colonna-Dashwood**, Co-owner, Colonna and Small's, UK Barista Champion 2012 & 2014

This vital ingredient is the foundation of every cup of coffee you have ever tasted, apart from the bean itself of course.

It's not just coffee that relies so dramatically on this everyday and seemingly straightforward substance. The worlds of craft beer and whiskey are suitable comparisons, with breweries and distilleries proudly signifying the provenance of their water as being a vital part of their product.

A roaster, though, sells coffee, the water bit comes post sale. The water will be different and unique based on the locality of brewing, and this is on top of all of the other variables that define coffee brewing such as grinding, temperature and brew ratios. The reality is that the impact of water is rarely directly witnessed, with the other variables often being seen as the cause for dramatic flavor changes. You may be wondering right now, how big an impact can it really have?

I'm yet to present the same coffee brewed with different waters to drinkers and not have them exclaim 'I can't believe how different they are, they taste like different coffees'. These aren't 'coffee people' either, but customers who contested prior to the tasting that 'you may be able to taste the difference but I doubt I can tell.'

It may make you question whether the coffee that you tried and weren't particularly keen on, was a representative version of what the bean actually tastes like, or at the least what it is capable of tasting of like.

So, why the big difference, what is in the water?

Nearly all water that trickles out of a tap or sits in a bottle is not just water. As well as the $H2O$ there are other bits and bobs in the water. Minerals mainly. These have a big impact not only on what we extract from the coffee but also how that flavor sits in the cup of coffee.

It's fair to say that currently the way the coffee industry discusses water is through the use of a measurement called Total Dissolved Solids (TDS).

TDS has become the measurement which is relied upon to distinguish and inform us about how water will affect our coffee. It gives us a total of everything in the water. The problem though, is that TDS doesn't tell us everything we need to know about the water; it doesn't tell us about what those solids are. On top of this, TDS meters don't measure some non-solids that have a huge impact on flavor.

In the water, we need the minerals calcium and magnesium to help pull out a lot of the desirable flavor in the coffee, but we also need the right amount of buffering ability in the water to balance the acids. This buffering ability can be noted as the bicarbonate content of the water.

So for example an 'empty' soft water with no minerals will lack flavor complexity and the lack of buffer will mean a more vinegary acidity.

However the coffee shops in this guide will most likely have a trick up their sleeve. The industry filtration systems that have been developed primarily to stop scale build up in the striking and valuable espresso machines, also produce water compositions that are more often than not preferable for coffee brewing. Speciality coffee shops require all manner of specifics to be obsessed over and carefully executed. That cup of coffee that hits you and stops you in your step with intense, balanced and complex flavor will owe its

brilliance to careful brewing, a knowledgeable brewer and superb equipment. However, it also owes a significant part of its beautiful character and flavor to the water it is brewed with.

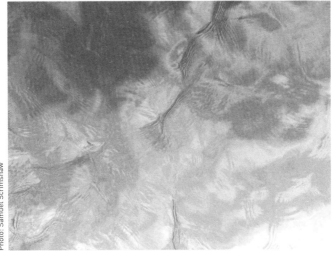

Photo: Samuel Scrimshaw

The Coffee Taster's Flavor Wheel

by **Peter Giuliano**, Chief Research Officer, Specialty Coffee Association

The Coffee Taster's Flavor Wheel has its roots in the World Coffee Research (WCR) Coffee Lexicon project, a piece of scientific research seeking to identify the most common and distinctive flavors that occur in coffee. Over the course of a year, World Coffee Research and the Specialty Coffee Association (SCA) gathered hundreds of samples of coffee, which were analyzed in the Center for Sensory Analysis at Kansas State University. This project identified 110 unique attributes present in coffee and resulted in the publication of the WCR Sensory Lexicon. From there, SCA went to the Food Science and Technology department of UC Davis, where researchers designed a unique, sophisticated sensory research project to understand how tasters organized taste attributes, leading to the design of the SCA/WCR Coffee Taster's Flavor Wheel.

In all, the Coffee Taster's Flavor Wheel is the product of the largest collaborative coffee sensory science research project in history and reflects the work of dozens of coffee tasters and sensory scientists over hundreds of hours. The Coffee Taster's Flavor Wheel is used by coffee professionals every day to help evaluate and describe coffee's tastes, flavors and aromas. The wheel has been translated into 10 languages and is seen in tasting rooms and sensory laboratories all over the world.

How to use the wheel

Though the Coffee Taster's Flavor Wheel is based in rigorous research and sensory science, it is easy for even a novice to use. The flavors (called 'attributes') are arranged on the wheel according to how coffee tasters actually use them making the use of the wheel very intuitive. The trick is to begin at the center: after tasting a coffee, simply begin by identifying a flavor in one of the 9 'first tier' attributes in the innermost level of the wheel. Say you choose 'fruity'. From there, the taster choses one of the 4 'second tier' attributes. Say you choose 'citrus fruit'. From there, you can choose among four specific citrus fruits. In this way, the taster moves from general to specific tastes, helping zero in on specific attributes in a methodical but simple way.

The Coffee Taster's Flavor Wheel© encourages coffee lovers of all kinds to enjoy and make use of this valuable tool. To learn more, visit **www.sca.coffee**.

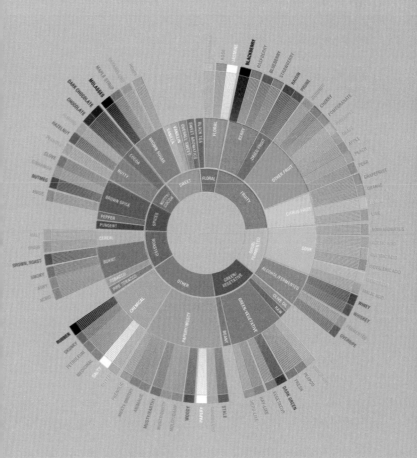

COFFEE TASTER'S FLAVOR WHEEL CREATED USING THE SENSORY
LEXICON DEVELOPED BY WORLD COFFEE RESEARCH
© 2016 SCA AND WCR

v.2

Brewing Coffee at Home

by **Christian Baker, David Robson, Sam Mason & The New York Coffee Guide**

Y ou may be surprised to know that coffee brewed at home can rival that of your favorite coffee shop. All you need is good quality ingredients and some inexpensive equipment. Keep in mind that small variations in grind coarseness, coffee/water ratio and brew time will make a significant difference to flavor, and that trial and error is the key to unlocking perfection.

Whole Beans: Whole bean coffee is superior to pre-ground. Coffee rapidly deteriorates once ground, so buy your coffee in whole bean form and store it in an air-tight container at room temperature. It should be consumed between three and thirty days after roast and ground only moments before brewing.

Water: Water is important because it makes up over 98% of the finished drink. Only use bottled water, preferably with a dry residue between 80-150mg/l. It will inhibit your ability to extract flavor and reveal only a fraction of a coffee's potential.

Digital scales: Get a set of scales accurate to 1g and large enough to hold your coffee brewer. Coffee is commonly measured in 'scoops' or 'tablespoons', but coffee and water are best measured by weight for greater accuracy and to ensure repeatability. Small changes in the ratio of coffee to water can have a significant impact on flavor. A good starting point is 60-70g of coffee per litre of water. Apply this ratio to meet the size of your brewer.

Grinder

A burr grinder is essential. Burr grinders are superior to blade grinders because they allow the grind coarseness to be set and produce a more consistent size of coffee fragment (critical for an even extraction). As a general rule, the coarser the grind the longer the brew time required, and vice versa. For example, an espresso needs a very fine grind whereas a French Press works with a coarser grind.

French Press

Preheat the French Press with hot water, and discard. Add 34g of coarsely ground coffee and pour in 500g of water just below boiling point (201-203°F). Steep for 4 to 5 minutes then gently plunge to the bottom. Decant the coffee straight away to avoid over-brewing (known as over-extraction).

AeroPress

The AeroPress is wonderfully versatile. It can be used with finely ground coffee and a short steep time, or with a coarser grind and a longer steep time. The latter is our preferred method for its flavor and repeatability. Preheat the AeroPress using hot water, and discard. Rinse the paper filter before securing, and place the AeroPress over a sturdy cup or jug. Add 16g of coffee and pour in 240g of water at 203°F. Secure the plunger on top, creating a seal. Steep for 3 minutes then plunge over 20 seconds.

Pour Over

We recommend using a pouring kettle for better pouring control. Place a filter paper in the cone and rinse through with hot water. Add 15g of coffee and slowly pour 30g of 203°F water to pre-soak the coffee grounds. This creates the 'bloom'. After 30 seconds add 250g of water, pouring steadily in a circular motion over the center. It should take 1 minute and 45 seconds to pour and between 30-45 seconds to drain through. The key is to keep the flow of water steady. If the water drains too quickly/slowly, adjust the coarseness of the grind to compensate.

Stovetop

A stovetop will not make an espresso, it will, however, make a strong coffee. Pour hot water in to the base to the fill-line or just below the pressure release valve. Fill the basket with ground coffee of medium coarseness (between Pour Over and French Press). Traditional wisdom suggests a fine grind in pursuit of espresso, but stovetops extract differently to espresso machines and grinding fine is a recipe for bitter, over-extracted coffee. Screw the base to the top and place on the heat. When you hear bubbling, remove immediately and decant to ensure the brewing has stopped.

Illustrations: Zoë Barker

Traditional Pump Espresso Machine

Traditional pump espresso machines are ideal for that barista experience to create espresso-based coffee at home. Coffee should be freshly and finely ground and dosed into single or double shot filter baskets. It is then tamped to extract full flavor aroma and coffee crema. The machine controls temperature for a more consistent cup. To enjoy milk drinks such as flat whites and cappuccinos simply froth fresh milk using the steam wand (stay below 158°F) and top up your espresso.

Bean to Cup Machine

Bean to Cup provides the perfect 'coffee shop' fix and fast. It gives you all the versatility of choice and personalization of a traditional pump machine. At the touch of a button, it burr-grinds fresh beans and froths milk (some machines even have a built in carafe), creating a fresh taste for your cup. You can personalize the strength, length, temperature, and even the froth setting. One-touch drink options make your personalized coffee time and again, without mess or fuss.

Latte Art

by **Jai Lott**, Coffee Director for Bluestone Lane

Latte art is the barista's signature in a milk based espresso drink.

Over the years latte art has shifted from being 'etched' chocolate sauce designs and foamy 'hand spooned' structures, to a fragile and carefully constructed pattern where the slightest movement of the hand can make or break a masterpiece.

There are 3 major components to world-class latte art: espresso, milk and execution.

1 Espresso

Perfect espresso is your canvas. Well-executed fresh extraction with a thick stable crema sets the foundation for your latte art. A double shot or around 40 grams of yield and medium roast is a great starting point. This helps create contrast in the cup. Espresso and milk preparation should happen simultaneously to ensure crema does not have time to dissipate.

2 Milk

The colder your milk, the better. This gives it more chances at rotation in the pitcher before reaching temperature, which in turn increases your milk's texture. Once the steam wand is in position slightly below the surface of the milk and sits slightly off center, engage the wand and slowly lower the jug adding small amounts of air while simultaneously keeping the milk spinning solid. All air should be added prior to the milk reaching room temperature for great results. Turn off the steam when you reach your desired temperature.

Ideal learning tools:

- A steaming pitcher that has perfect spout symmetry. Using the same jug every time is vital to getting comfortable with latte art.

- A wide ceramic cup of around 8oz is great to start with. This gives you plenty of breathing space.

- An environment where you can concentrate and not be bumped!

3 Execution

If everything worked out (and trust me it takes practice even getting to this point) you should have beautiful espresso and a hot pitcher with milk resembling freshly applied paint. Its time to pour!

Tilting the cup at 45 degrees, pour into the center of the espresso at a height of 2-3 inches. Imagine a diving board and a diver trying to pierce the espresso without disrupting the surface. Keep an even flow for the entire pour.

Once the cup gets to the low edge of the cup, two things need to happen:

Firstly, flatten out the cup while simultaneously bringing the pitcher all the way down to almost full contact with the espresso. This will increase the amount of microfoam allowed from behind the pitchers spout and a white dot will begin to appear (remember keep the same flow the whole time!).

Secondly, in the final moment of the pour, exit the cup by lifting the jug and cutting through the center of your white dot. Imagine the milk from the spout is an airplane taking off.

Perfect love heart!

Once you master our love hearts, move on to a two-stack tulip.

The big secret - stick to one design for days, weeks if needed. Get each design mastered before progressing to the next. This is the way to get good fast and an understanding of what each movement will result in.

Spill milk, make a mess and most importantly have fun! That's what coffee should be all about. Just don't forget that latte art certainly makes coffee look great, but great espresso and milk are more important!

Education & Training

by **Allie Caran**, Director of Education, Toby's Estate Coffee Roasters

One of the greatest achievements in the advancement of Specialty Coffee has been its impressive growth of coffee education. In the past decade we have witnessed the research, development and implementation of standardized coffee education on a world-wide level. Organizations such as the Specialty Coffee Association (SCA) have spearheaded the conversation by representing individuals throughout the coffee supply chain, creating a cohesive shared experience and an impressive global network.

For those looking to learn more about coffee, or ultimately to create a greater depth of knowledge, the SCA offers pathways like the New Coffee Skills Program. These programs offer both industry professionals and consumers a way to explore various aspects of coffee; brewing, sensory skills, and even roasting. With education being at the forefront of coffee, many roasteries have created similar models of educational classes and certifications.

When Toby's Estate opened in 2012, there was a recognized lack of educational resources for coffee professionals and consumers alike. We built two state-of-the-art Coffee Labs and selected the industry's best coffee leaders to educate both baristas and coffee lovers.

Our Coffee Educators continually foster a culture of curiosity and knowledge, providing a thoughtful and focused forum for learning that includes hands-on practice as well as theory. Similar to the New Coffee Skills Program, students can choose to hone-in and learn more about any specific topic in the world of coffee in a private class setting; brewing, sustainability, green buying, and sensory analysis. Additionally, we offer an in-house Certification Program for baristas. Upon completion of all modules, baristas are tested in both written and practical formats to assess written comprehension and technical expertise in coffee, giving them the tools they needed to be exceptional Coffee Professionals.

Our program, like many, revolves around the advancement of knowledge in coffee. It is an experience open to anyone and everyone. As the industry continues to evolve, education and shared knowledge will be the keystone to successful growth.

Espresso

by **Bill McAllister**, Director of the Service Department, Irving Farm New York

The definition of espresso is a method of brewing coffee according to the Specialty Coffee Association of America, a trade group that represents and undoubtedly has some direct connection to every person and place in this book. Yet the difference between a coffee made using a Chemex versus a vacuum pot or any other coffee maker is negligible compared to what an espresso machine produces. The root cause is pressure. Espresso machines take water that would normally be poured or sprinkled onto coffee and forces it through the pressure of the atmosphere. But who came up with that? How did they know it could make coffee so much more delicious than normal?

The etymology of espresso reveals a lot about the intention of this technology. If we Anglicize the word into 'expresso', it is easy to see that the drink needs to be made quickly, but also that it needs to be made expressly for a consumer. Back in Italian, it's just as easily interpreted as 'to press out', bringing pressure back into the picture. Put it all together, and you have a device that makes coffee quickly, one at a time, using pressure. All of this is according to Andrea Illy (yes, that Illy) as written in Espresso Coffee, one of the few textbooks on coffee.

It paints a somewhat primitive picture of Italy in the 1880s, where the first patents for espresso machines are traced. The technology at the time was coarse and rugged. It relied on huge boilers heated by fire that used a head of steam to push water through the ground coffee. A barista would be hard-pressed to make anything that wasn't quite bitter. This was espresso for decades. But then, manufacturers introduced a lever and piston as an alternative method of generating pressure. This change allowed the machines to be much smaller, brew at pressures that have become today's standard, and use water that isn't super-heated. All of a sudden espresso carts became a reality, bringing the means of caffeination to even more people. But the most important part of the change in the machines is that it is no longer impossible for a shot to be pulled that is more than something used as a dose of energy.

The espresso of today and its potential to be mind-blowingly delicious has a culture surrounding it that elevates it above the rest of coffee. Cafes have moved far beyond just dishing out shots to give workers a boost mid-afternoon. A coffee shop that wants to be the talk of the town these days draws customers in by talking about the specific farms their coffee is from, the agronomy of the plant from which the coffee is harvested, and a level of precision that requires scales that wouldn't be out of place in a display on St Marks Place.

How we went from pre-industrial caffeine machines relying on levers and pistons to today's models doesn't contain any big eureka moments, but is mostly a steady stream of smart revisions. Baristas realized early on that their ability to reliably make the most delicious espresso they've tasted required having a machine they could count on to work the same way every time. To this end, springs and levers were replaced by electric pumps and gas burners were replaced by heating elements controlled by computers.

Yet with all of these, advances were driven by the trial and error of passionate baristas, because despite the long history of espresso, there is not a lot of scientific writing about the process with which it is made. When a handful of videos featuring clear plastic portafilters started trickling out in the last few years, coffee pros everywhere were astounded - the first real evidence in over a century as to what's happening when making espresso!

Explanations of how and why espresso works may be lacking, but we can still gather a few lessons as consumers. A properly prepared shot looks elegant as it pours into a cup, flowing thick but steady, like warm honey, a promise of flavor that delivers on the intoxicating smell characteristic of coffee shops everywhere. At its best, a coffee brewed as espresso sees its flavors held under a magnifying glass. The experience is intense, but often divisive: fruity Ethiopian coffees taste like someone plopped jam in the bottom of your demitasse, so lush with fruit flavor and sweetness it seems impossible that the only ingredient is coffee. The second you sip a good espresso, all thoughts of history are fleeting memories; you thoughts are now on the delicious beverage in your hands.

Coffee Glossary

Acidity: the pleasant tartness of a coffee. Examples of acidity descriptors include lively and flat. One of the principal attributes evaluated by professional tasters when determining the quality of a coffee.

AeroPress: a hand-powered coffee brewer marketed by Aerobie Inc., and launched in 2005. Consists of two cylinders, one sliding within the other, somewhat resembling a large syringe. Water is forced through ground coffee held in place by a paper filter, creating a concentrated filter brew.

Affogato: one or more scoops of vanilla ice cream topped with a shot of espresso, served as a dessert.

Americano, Caffè Americano: a long coffee consisting of espresso with hot water added on top. Originates from the style of coffee favored by American GIs stationed in Europe during WWII.

Arabica, Coffea arabica: the earliest cultivated species of coffee tree and the most widely grown, Arabica accounts for approximately 70% of the world's coffee. Superior in quality to Robusta, it is more delicate and is generally grown at higher altitudes.

Aroma: the fragrance produced by brewed coffee. Examples of aroma descriptors include earthy, spicy and floral. One of the principal attributes evaluated by professional tasters when determining the quality of a coffee.

Barista: a professional person skilled in making coffee, particularly one working at an espresso bar.

Blend: a combination of coffees from different countries or regions. Mixed together, they achieve a balanced flavor profile no single coffee can offer alone.

Body: describes the heaviness, thickness or relative weight of coffee on the tongue. One of the principal attributes evaluated by professional tasters when determining the quality of a coffee.

Bottomless portafilter, naked portafilter: a portafilter without spouts, allowing espresso to flow directly from the bottom of the filter basket into the cup. Allows the extraction to be monitored visually.

Brew group: the assembly protruding from the front of an espresso machine consisting of the grouphead, portafilter and basket. The brew group must be heated to a sufficient temperature to produce a good espresso.

Brew pressure: pressure of 9 bar is required for espresso extraction.

Brew temperature: the water temperature at the point of contact with coffee. Optimum brew temperature varies by extraction method. Espresso brew temperature is typically 194-203°F. A stable brew temperature is crucial for good espresso.

Brew time, extraction time: the contact time between water and coffee. Espresso brew time is typically 25-30 seconds. Brew times are dictated by a variety of factors including the grind coarseness and degree of roast.

Burr set: an integral part of a coffee grinder. Consists of a pair of rotating steel discs between which coffee beans are ground. Burrs are either flat or conical in shape.

Café con leche: a traditional Spanish coffee consisting of espresso topped with scalded milk.

Caffeine: an odorless, slightly bitter alkaloid responsible for the stimulating effect of coffee.

Cappuccino: a classic Italian coffee comprising espresso, steamed milk and topped with a layer of foam. Traditionally served in a 6oz cup and sometimes topped with powdered chocolate or cinnamon.

Capsule: a self-contained, pre-ground, pre-pressed portion of coffee, individually sealed inside a plastic capsule. Capsule brewing systems are commonly found in domestic coffee machines. Often compatible only with certain equipment brands.

Chemex: A type of pour over coffee brewer with a distinctive hourglass-shaped vessel. Invented in 1941, the Chemex has become regarded as a design classic and is on permanent display at the Museum of Modern Art in New York City.

Cherry: the fruit of the coffee plant. Each cherry contains two coffee seeds (beans).

Cold brew: Cold brew refers to the process of steeping coffee grounds in room temperature or cold water for an extended period. Cold brew coffee is not to be confused with iced coffee.

Cortado: a traditional short Spanish coffee consisting of espresso cut with a small quantity of steamed milk. Similar to an Italian piccolo.

Crema: the dense caramel-colored layer that forms on the surface of an espresso. Consists of emulsified oils created by the dispersion of gases in liquid at high pressure. The presence of crema is commonly equated with a good espresso.

Cupping: a method by which professional tasters perform sensory evaluation of coffee. Hot water is poured over ground coffee and left to extract. The taster first samples the aroma, then tastes the coffee by slurping it from a spoon.

Decaffeinated: coffee with approximately 97% or more of its naturally occurring caffeine removed is classified as decaffeinated.

Dispersion screen, shower screen: a component of the grouphead that ensures even distribution of brewing water over the coffee bed in the filter basket.

Dosage: the mass of ground coffee used for a given brewing method. Espresso dosage is typically 7-10g of ground coffee (14-20g for a double).

Double espresso, doppio: typically 30-50ml extracted from 14-20g of ground coffee. The majority of coffee venues in this guide serve double shots as standard.

Drip method: a brewing method that allows brew water to seep through a bed of ground coffee by gravity, not pressure.

Espresso: the short, strong shot of coffee that forms the basis for many other coffee beverages. Made by forcing hot water at high pressure through a compressed bed of finely ground coffee.

Espresso machine: in a typical configuration, a pump delivers hot water from a boiler to the brew group, where it is forced under pressure through ground coffee held in the portafilter. A separate boiler delivers steam for milk steaming.

Extraction: the process of infusing coffee with hot water to release flavor, accomplished either by allowing ground coffee to sit in hot water for a period of time or by forcing hot water through ground coffee under pressure.

Fifth Wave / 5th Wave™: A new era for the coffee industry signifying the creation of 'boutique at scale'. This means aspiring to and achieving the highest quality of output across one's business or café, including, but not limited to, atmosphere, coffee quality, service level, staff training, business and IT systems. This era represents an advance on previous 'waves' most notably the 3rd Wave or artisan coffee era typified by craft coffee, or The 4th Wave, the science of coffee. 5th Wave businesses tend to be aspirational, professionally run businesses targeting a savvy millennial audience.

Filter method: any brewing method in which water filters through a bed of ground coffee. Most commonly used to describe drip method brewers that use a paper filter to separate grounds from brewed coffee.

Flat white: an espresso-based beverage first made popular in Australia and New Zealand. Made with a double shot of espresso with finely steamed milk and a thin layer of microfoam. Typically served as a 5-6oz drink with latte art.

Flavor: the way a coffee tastes. Flavor descriptors include nutty and earthy. One of the principal attributes evaluated by professional tasters when determining the quality of a coffee.

French press, plunger pot, cafetiere: a brewing method that separates grounds from brewed coffee by pressing them to the bottom of the brewing receptacle with a mesh filter attached to a plunger.

Green coffee, green beans: unroasted coffee. The dried seeds from the coffee cherry.

Grind: the degree of coarseness to which coffee beans are ground. A crucial factor in determining the nature of a coffee brew. Grind coarseness should be varied in accordance with the brewing method. Methods involving longer brew times call for a coarse grind. A fine grind is required for brew methods with a short extraction time such as espresso.

Grinder: a vital piece of equipment for making coffee. Coffee beans must be ground evenly for a good extraction. Most commonly motorised, but occasionally manual. Burr grinders are the best choice for an even grind.

Group: see Brew Group

Grouphead: a component of the brew group containing the locking connector for the portafilter and the dispersion screen.

Honey process, pulped natural, semi-washed: a method of processing coffee where the cherry is removed (pulped), but the beans are sun-dried with mucilage intact. Typically results in a sweet flavor profile with a balanced acidity.

Latte, caffè latte: an Italian beverage made with espresso combined with steamed milk, traditionally topped with foamed milk and served in a glass. Typically at least 8oz in volume, usually larger.

Latte art: the pattern or design created by pouring steamed milk on top of espresso. Only finely steamed milk is suitable for creating latte art. Popular patterns include the rosetta and heart.

Lever espresso machine: lever machines use manual force to drive a piston that generates the pressure required for espresso extraction. Common in the first half of the 20th century, but now largely superseded by electric pump-driven machines.

Long black: a coffee beverage made by adding an espresso on top of hot water. Similar to an Americano, but usually shorter and the crema is preserved.

Macchiato: a coffee beverage consisting of espresso 'stained' with a dash of steamed milk (espresso macchiato) or a tall glass of steamed milk 'stained' with espresso (latte macchiato).

Matcha: Finely ground powder of specially grown and processed green tea. The matcha plants are shade-grown for three weeks before harvest.

Microfoam: the preferred texture of finely-steamed milk for espresso-based coffee drinks. Essential for pouring latte art. Achieved by incorporating a lesser quantity of air during the milk steaming process.

Micro-lot coffee: coffee originating from a small, discrete area within a farm, typically benefiting from conditions favorable to the development of a particular set of characteristics. Micro-lot coffees tend to fetch higher prices due to their unique nature.

Mocha, caffè mocha: similar to a caffè latte, but with added chocolate syrup or powder.

Natural process: a simple method of processing coffee where whole cherries (with the bean inside) are dried on raised beds under the sun. Typically results in a lower acidity coffee with a heavier body and exotic flavors.

Over extracted: describes coffee with a bitter or burnt taste, resulting from ground coffee exposed to hot water for too long.

Peaberry: a small, round coffee bean formed when only one seed, rather than the usual two, develops in a coffee cherry. Peaberry beans produce a different flavor profile, typically lighter-bodied with higher acidy.

Piccolo: a short Italian coffee beverage made using espresso topped with an equal quantity of steamed milk. Traditionally served in a glass.

Pod: a self-contained, pre-ground, pre-pressed puck of coffee, individually wrapped inside a perforated paper filter. Mostly found in domestic espresso machines. Often compatible only with certain equipment brands.

Pour over: a type of drip filter method in which a thin, steady stream of water is poured slowly over a bed of ground coffee contained within a filter cone.

Pouring kettle: a kettle with a narrow swan-neck spout specifically designed to deliver a steady, thin stream of water.

Portafilter: consists of a handle (usually plastic) attached to a metal cradle that holds the filter basket. Inserted into the group head and locked in place in preparation for making an espresso. Usually features a single or double spout on the underside to direct the flow of coffee into a cup.

Portafilter basket: a flat bottomed, bowl-shaped metal insert that sits in the portafilter and holds a bed of ground coffee. The basket has an array of tiny holes in the base allowing extracted coffee to seep through and pour into a cup.

Puck: immediately after an espresso extraction, the bed of spent coffee grounds forms compressed waste matter resembling a small hockey puck.

Pull: the act of pouring an espresso. The term originates from the first half of the 20th century when manual machines were the norm, and baristas pulled a lever to create an espresso.

Ristretto: a shorter 'restricted' shot of espresso. Made using the same dose and brew time as for a regular espresso, but with less water. The result is a richer and more intense beverage.

Roast: the process by which green coffee is heated in order to produce coffee beans ready for consumption. Caramelization occurs as intense heat converts starches in the bean to simple sugars, imbuing the bean with flavor and transforming its color to a golden brown.

Robusta, Coffea canephora: the second most widely cultivated coffee species after arabica, robusta accounts for approximately 30% of the world's coffee. Robusta is hardier and grown at lower altitudes than arabica. It has a much higher caffeine content than arabica, and a less refined flavor. Commonly used in instant coffee blends.

Shot: a single unit of brewed espresso.

Single origin, single estate: coffee from one particular region or farm.

Siphon brewer, vacuum brewer: an unusual brewing method that relies on the action of a vacuum to draw hot water through coffee from one glass chamber to another. The resulting brew is remarkably clean.

Small batch: refers to roasting beans in small quantities, typically between 4-24kg, but sometimes larger.

Speciality coffee: a premium quality coffee scoring 80 points or above (from a total of 100) in the SCAA grading scale.

Steam wand: the protruding pipe found on an espresso machine that supplies hot steam used to froth and steam milk.

Stovetop, moka pot: a brewing method that makes strong coffee (but not espresso). Placed directly on a heat source, hot water is forced by steam pressure from the lower chamber to the upper chamber, passing through a bed of coffee.

Tamp: the process of distributing and pressing ground coffee into a compact bed within the portafilter basket in preparation for brewing espresso. The degree of pressure applied during tamping is a key variable in espresso extraction. Too light and the brew water will percolate rapidly (tending to under extract), too firm and the water flow will be impeded (tending to over extract).

Tamper: the small pestle-like tool used to distribute and compact ground coffee in the filter basket.

Third wave coffee: the movement that treats coffee as an artisanal foodstuff rather than a commodity product. Quality coffee reflects its terroir, in a similar manner to wine.

Under extracted: describes coffee that has not been exposed to brew water for long enough. The resulting brew is often sour and thin-bodied.

V60: a popular type of pour over coffee brewer marketed by Hario. The product takes its name from the 60° angle of the V-shaped cone. Typically used to brew one or two cups only.

Washed process: one of the most common methods of processing coffee cherries. Involves fermentation in tanks of water to remove mucilage. Typically results in a clean and bright flavor profile with higher acidity.

Whole bean: coffee that has been roasted but not ground.

A-Z List of Coffee Venues

Notes, sketches, phone numbers etc.